Quote Me On This

The Wit and Wisdom of Coleman Cox

Coleman Cox

Edited by Karl W. Palachuk

Great Little Book Publishing Co., Inc
2121 Natomas Crossing Dr., #200
Sacramento, CA 95834

Quote Me On This – The Wit and Wisdom of Coleman Cox by Coleman Cox. Edited by Karl W. Palachuk.

Printed in the United States of America.

www.greatlittlebook.com

5 4 3 2 1
ISBN 978-0-9763760-3-3

Contents

Acknowledgements

As with any project, this book came about because of the efforts of many people. First on this list is Svetlana Shurayev. Lana did a lot of research to determine whether we had all the source materials we wanted, as well as doing all the scanning and some of the copy editing for the book. Thank you, Lana!

I thank Connie Kong for the cover design. And, of course, thanks go out to Stephanie Martindale for the layout of this book. Stephanie has always done a great job for us and we're happy to have her on this project.

I thank my wife Laura for her support in this new venture. She never looks at my projects and asks "Is that going to make money?" or "Is that a smart thing to do?" No, Laura just looks at my projects and says "What are you up to now?"

Editor's Introduction

By Karl W. Palachuk

Welcome to the Coleman Cox collection, produced by Great Little Book Publishing Co., Inc. We are very pleased and honored to be reprinting this material.

Coleman Cox is an intriguing character. He is both inspiring and humorous. One can easily imagine him handing out sage advice with a smirk on his face. I imagine him to be a great story-teller and a wonderful dinner guest.

I first stumbled upon Coleman Cox because of one of my hobbies. I love great quotations. That's why my Relax Focus Succeed® web site is filled with them. I sprinkle them in my newsletter and post them on the "Pith Page" at www.relaxfocussucceed.com.

One cannot collect great quotations for very long without finding some great one-liners by Coleman Cox. His favorite topic is sales, but he also covers business in general and life in general.

After stumbling across his quotes time and time again, I decided to go looking for his books. But I didn't find books; I found booklets. Lots and lots of booklets. Cox's titles were short and pithy, like most of his quotes. The titles included "Take It From Me," "Listen to This," and "Just Plain Talk."

Cox's writing started in 1921 when he decided to print up a small paper booklet with a thick paper cover. As he tells it, this booklet consisted of "a few hundred paragraphs telling something of my experiences and observations during thirty years of active business life."

He gave away a few thousand of these booklets. After that he received hundreds of letters requesting multiple copies of the booklet. So he printed a second edition, which sold out before the printing was complete. After that the booklet quickly went to a third, fourth, fifth printing, and beyond.

Within ten months, "Take It From Me," the first booklet, had sold millions of copies. So, in 1922 Cox came out with another brilliant collection of witticisms. Every copy was sold out before the printing of the first edition was complete.

It didn't take long for Cox to realize that these millions of little booklets were being purchased by business owners as gifts for their employees and clients. Because Cox could easily print off small runs, he offered to print up booklets with a customized message in the front. These messages are often quite heartfelt and are obviously written by business owners striving for a better world.

In one customized copy of "Just Plain Talk," O.R. Peterson writes to his clients:

> We have come to realize that we owe each other some expression for whatever success we have attained and possibly this little book will mean quite as much to you as it does to us.
>
> Cox's little paragraphs are inspiring and entertaining. Turn to any page and you'll find yourself flipping through several more. You'll be asking yourself "What will he say next?"

At the same time, although these words are from eight decades ago, they ring true today. Other than the fact that business is no longer completely dominated by men, almost nothing here is outdated. Occasionally there's a reference to "the young ladies" that wouldn't fly too far in modern conversation. But virtually everything else fits very well in our society.

I have removed only a few paragraphs, and modernized only a dozen or so. The remainder is just as Cox wrote it more than eighty years ago.

I'm sure you'll find a great deal to enjoy here. And you'll be quoting Coleman Cox for a long time to come.

> "It is my hope that some one or more of my little paragraphs will have something to do with the making of your tomorrows more happy and successful than your yesterdays."

- Coleman Cox

1
Take It From Me

"Every man, be he employer, employee or unemployed, will find himself mentioned on more pages than one."

- From Coleman Cox's introduction to the
Eighth Edition of Take It From Me

These little paragraphs like the Ten Commandments are not supposed to apply to you.

You can't buy Confidence and Respect with Profanity and Vulgarity.

You will nearly always find a prospect in the mental attitude you expected to find him in.

It takes more than vaselined hair and a barbershop manicure to make you a polished gentleman.

Of course your boss doesn't run his business right. Probably he would fire you if he did.

When the boss asks you what you think about a matter, tell him what you think, and not what you think he thinks.

An expense account offers you the best opportunity to convince your employer you are Economical, Honest and Truthful.

Never lose the respect of those you are employed by, or those you are working with, by asking for an advance or a loan.

There are a lot of fellows waiting to take the man's job who says "it can't be done," or "they can't be sold."

The surest way to get commuters to read office bulletins is to paste them on the clock at 4:45 every afternoon.

Some men never read the Bible—because they didn't write it.

It is not what you say, but how you say it, who you say it to and when, that gets the order.

You are well dressed when no one can remember anything you are wearing.

The man who is looking for a job and wages is being given the preference over the fellows looking for a position and a salary.

Another good thing about telling the truth is, you don't have to remember what you say.

The old saw says every man has his price. That may not be true, but when I see an employee sacrifice the good will of a customer for a momentary gain I think, "surely that man's price is small."

Auto speedsters, like the hurry-up salesmen, often land in the ditch. This would be just retribution were it not for the fact that they often injure others by their foolish haste.

The boss is always glad to see the fellow back from his vacation who is glad to get back.

More applications for positions these days carry the line "I own my own car" than "I own my own home."

All some employees have on their minds is what they have on their backs.

It is not every man who knows how to handle dynamite, authority, T. N. T. and prosperity.

Spend five minutes every day thinking of some good you can do someone—then do it.

A woman with a sharp tongue will soon cut herself off the payroll.

A want ad for an office boy brought many applicants. One little fellow gave the young lady at the information desk a scribbled note for immediate delivery to the boss, which when opened read, "I'm the last kid in the line. Don't do anything until you see me." He got the job. He used his head.

"Never mind the business outlook. Be on the lookout for business."

The fellow who tries the most pools generally catches more fish than the man who uses up a lot of time looking for the good places.

Dawgone a man that can't look you in the eye when you are talking to him.

Don't forget you are a part of the organization just as much as the bass drum is a part of the orchestra — likewise, don't forget that bass drum solos are rather monotonous.

"Don't worry when you stumble. Remember a worm is about the only thing that can't fall down."

A smile on the face of some salespeople often reminds me of the top layer of apples in a box, or berries in a basket.

Loud talk makes noise, not sales.

The longer you listen to some employees talk, the more thoroughly you become convinced that all the bull is not put out from Durham, North Carolina.

The first man you must sell on the value of your goods is yourself.

A small employee might grow in the right environment. If he does, his salary will increase in the same proportion—and don't forget that a man makes his own environment.

Many manufacturing concerns' greatest come from by-products. Employee, your by-product is your idle time. What profit are you getting out of it?

When a prospect looks at his watch—look for your hat.

Tombstones are cold and cheerless. Yet they always have a good word for everyone under them.

Prospective buyers don't pay rent or salaries. The salesman who talks much about his prospective business is usually trying to camouflage the fact that he did little or nothing last month.

The bill collector who rings a bell while standing on a door mat bearing the word "Welcome," feels he is above lying.

The fellow with steady habits and a steady tongue always has a steady job.

We have all met men who were too little to be big. You know the fellow I mean, the one who mooches lunches, smokes, gum, etc., and walks ten blocks in the middle of a busy day to save car fare.

You will always find at least one durn fool in a crowded elevator who thinks politeness consists of blocking the exit until the lady in the rear elbows her way through the crowd.

If you have anything to say, say it, and with as few words as possible. That is what Abraham Lincoln did, and the world still remembers and repeats what he said.

Nothing is improved by anger except the arch of a cat's back.

Keeping salesmen's cars tired and the salesmen from getting tired makes many a business man want to retire.

Always be courteous in the face of discourtesy.

You'll get further by out-thinking a prospective buyer than you will by trying to out-talk him.

Say nothing when you have nothing to say, and keep on saying nothing when the prospect has something to say.

As a rule the boss does not pick men for advancement from the bunch of "Wind Jammers" who stand out in front waiting until the last minute to go in for work.

It's not what you would like to be, but what you are best fitted to do, that is going to get you somewhere in the business world.

Never say, "Well, I'll call again next week." Ask the prospective buyer to name a day and hour when you can see him. In other words, show him you place a value on your time and he will not feel he is throwing his away in talking to you.

Work will Win when Wishing Won't.

Good listeners make more sales than good talkers.

The young fellow who has a coffee and doughnut breakfast down in town, an armchair lunch, and eats a delicatessen dinner out of paper bags when he gets home in the evening, nine times out of ten has married some fool girl because she was a good dancer.

It is a good thing many employees are on the payroll at invoiced value in the place of their self-estimated worth, else their firms would go busted.

This old world is going to be a better place to live in when it becomes more generally known we suffer by our sins and not for our sins.

You are not dressed for work until you put on a smile.

There never was a better piece of advice than, "Don't make customers of your friends, but make friends of your customers."

Confidence is the backbone of all business. Don't do or say anything that would tend to destroy.

While climbing the ladder of success in business few men ever see the splinters, but take it from me, they feel 'em when they start sliding down.

Laugh, Love and Live Longer.

'Jever hear of a fellow working on a small salary crushing a woman's heart and being sued for breach of promise?

"Doesn't it make you sick to hear a millinery or ladies' suit saleswoman address a customer a dozen times a minute as 'My deah'?"

It was the employers of the country, and not the medical fraternity, who first discovered the symptoms of "hookworm" and "sleeping sickness."

Envy stands between many a man and success. Until you are a big enough man to honestly and sincerely glory in the promotion of a fellow worker—you'll never get far in the business world.

A Pullman porter when asked why rich men usually gave him small tips, while the poor men were liberal, answered, "Well sir, I don't know, except the rich man don't want nobody to know he's rich, and the poor man don't want nobody to know he's poor." If you have grasped the idea, we will move along to the next paragraph.

"It's the little things in life that count." The fellow that takes little interest in his work accomplishes but little, is paid but little and lasts but a little while.

Learn when to stop talking. You might talk him out of it.

All things come to those who wait—but, there's too durn many waiting.

The only time some employees ever think of "moving up in front" is when a street car conductor yells it in their ears.

When I hear a salesman boasting of the number of "calls" he makes a day I can't help thinking of a bell hop.

At an early morning hour an old ferryman was awakened by the call of someone wanting to cross the river. He answered, and received the reply, "Yes, sir, I want to cross the river, but I don't have any money." The ferryman replied, "Well, it makes damn little difference as to which side of the river you're on if you ain't got no money." This little fable is told to impress upon your mind the importance of investigating a man's credit before soliciting his business.

Arguments don't get orders and contracts. If you know your business well enough to explain it, there can be no room for argument.

Win respect by being respectable.

No man ever missed a train or lost an order by being a little ahead of time.

I have known many a promising young salesman to lose his job by promising.

There shouldn't be any law against shooting the fellow who in the course of a three-minute conversation will say, "sure," "see," "getme" or "zatso" a hundred times or more.

More than one man has been forced to make good because somebody made it harder for him to explain failure than work for success.

The use of flattery has flattened many a salesman's chance for an order.

In talking to a prospective buyer always imagine your boss is standing behind you listening to every word you are saying. Follow this rule and you will talk less, say more, make fewer promises and get further.

Take a firm interest in your firm's interests.

One morning I called up a big coal concern to give them the devil about not having delivered some coal as promised. As quick as the connection was made a most pleasing voice said, "Good morning! This is the Smith Coal Company speaking." The musical voice and happy "Good morning" of the operator took all the fight out of me and I was willing to agree the delay was excusable. The moral is, one of the most important workers in your office is your telephone operator.

The fellow who is always telling of the faults of others reminds me of the man with a pock-marked face who laughs at another's freckles.

When the "no trouble to show goods" and "money cheerfully refunded" signs come down you will know the truthful advertising law is in effect.

In speaking of the head of your company to strangers be sure to refer to him as "the old gent" or "the old man." It always adds dignity. You know what I mean.

A horse must be "broke" before he will work—Just so with some men.

Let a shave and a shine be your first morning investments.

The fewer favors you accept the less obligations you'll have to meet.

The fellow who comes to work whistling generally goes home singing.

Every salesroom should be equipped with a full length mirror with this suggestion hanging above it: "Before you go out to tell people you represent this firm look yourself over and see whether you do or not."

Since the passing of brass footrails and mahogany bars, many a business is made safe from the near salesman who threatened to ruin his firm by going over to a competitor if his pay check wasn't increased.

Remember, every man is entitled to his own religious and political belief and it's not up to you to change either.

When a man is chasing the almighty dollar he forgets there is a God, and when he is chasing women he forgets there is a devil.

Beware of the fellow whose one best reason for your giving him a job, or an order, is the fact that he belongs to the same church or fraternal society you do.

Leaving one prospect and walking several blocks to talk to another man of an entirely different type and under altogether different circumstances, has always proved just as restful to me as walking fifty yards.

Look your prospect in the eye when you are talking to him—and tell him the truth.

In asking the good Lord to give you luck enough to hold your job, always spell it with a "p."

Ten cents a day will keep a suit pressed.

Before you go to sleep tonight ask yourself if the firm you are with, and the world in general, is any better off because of your having lived another day.

Obtaining credit because you are associated with a firm that has a good reputation, and not paying your bills when they are due, is another good way to get fired.

Brighten up, when dark days come. If sales were good every day, business would become monotonous. The sun shines every day in Arizona, yet it has about the smallest population of any State in the Union.

A man's personal appearance has much to do with his business success. And, a man's business success has much to do with his personal appearance.

Few men ever made much money by dealing with their friends or relatives.

When you walk into a clean, well-kept office and see a picture of a mother and baby in a little silver frame occupying the center space on the desk, you can bet your last dime you have a mighty decent sort of man to talk with.

You have heard the "wise guy" and "smart Alex" salesmen tell of the schemes they worked, and the tricks they played to get in and see prospects, but few of them ever told you of their coming out with any signed contracts.

Truth is the best side-line you can carry.

Profiting by experience is using the knowledge you have gained through failures. In other words, it's converting failures into successes.

The song, "Don't bite the hand that's feeding you" should have been dedicated to the fellow who says unkind things about his employer.

Walk fast. A fire department looks just as much like business when answering a false alarm as it does when going to a real conflagration.

A lot of fellows lost their best alibi when whisky went out. Their relatives used to say they would have done wonders if the booze habit had not got them—now they are sober, but that is about all.

One time when I was trying to interest a carpet dealer in advertising, he said in a very gruff-like manner, "What do you know about carpets? You never laid a carpet in your life." I answered, with a smile, "No, and I never laid an egg, but I can tell you more about an egg omelet than any old hen that ever scratched for worms."

Jealousy causes many a man to lose his job.

Never object to a salesman taking an hour off to have his shoes half-soled, but have the can ready to tie to the fellow whose pants bag at the knees.

When you see a fellow leaving his office in the opposite direction from home, with a bouquet of roses and a box of candy, just take it from me that he is one of those fellows who has a wife that "doesn't understand him."

Henry Dodd says, "The reason most people do not recognize an opportunity when they meet it is because it usually goes around wearing overalls and looking like Hard Work."

Whether he did or not, let's all think Abraham Lincoln was addressing a salesmen's convention when he said, "You can fool some of the people all of the time, and all of the people some of the time, but you can't fool all the people all the time."

When you hear a man boast, "I say just what I think" just put it down that he doesn't think.

After a salesman has been massaging cement walks all day and has climbed steps high enough to shake hands with St. Peter, he can't work up much enthusiasm over a dancing party.

Take it from me it's bad business to take anyone with you when you are expecting to close a sale, for they are sure to "spill the beans." If they do not say something they shouldn't say right at the wrong time, it's ten to one they will get a foot hung in the cuspidor, kick over the waste paper basket, or lean back and break a leg off the chair.

Some employees let their wives buy whatever they want on credit because they would rather argue with bill collectors than with their wives.

"He profits most who serves best," says Rotary.

Initials are not names. Use your full name in business.

Goods left in the store-room or hidden behind the counter, are those that were sold by going over the manager's head to the boss.

Wine and whisky are about the only two things that improve with age, and they are with us no longer. I often think of this when I hear of a man boasting of the years he has held the same job. When you are not going ahead you are going back.

Win a man's confidence as quick as you can, and hold it as long as you can.

Some sales managers send out more misfits than clothing stores.

The fellow who works by the clock never earns the price of a watch.

When the man in the inner-office sends out word he is busy, write across the back of your card "That's why I'm calling; I've no time to waste on loafers." P. S. He'll see you.

Noisy dress has kept many a man from hearing a sales argument.

The boss will increase your salary when you increase his profits.

The cash register has saved more young men from ruin than all the ministers in the pulpits.

Doesn't a fellow feel all out of place when he walks into an office, dressed in a business suit, and finds himself facing a bunch of stenographers all dolled out in party dresses, cheeks painted, lips rouged and hair all fussed up?

The faults we see in others would seem small to us if we could but see our own.

It is not hard to believe some salesmen when they complain of being tired when night comes. Just think of how tired you would be if you had to listen to their talk all day as they do.

When you have had pointed out to you "a man who always has a good word for everybody," you don't have to look any farther in your search for one of the world's most hypocritical liars.

When you get the idea in your head that the world is against you—it is.

Don't make the mistake of thinking a prospect is believing all you are saying, simply because he does not call you a liar.

Any time a man marries for money—he earns it.

In talking business to a friend, look upon him as a stranger.

Some wives wear shiny silks while their husbands wear shiny suits.

The employer always has eye on the "I" man.

When your work becomes a task, quit, you're in the wrong business. Until your work is your pleasure you can never be successful.

When a man tells you he is not interested in your proposition say, with a smile, "I know you are not. That is why I have had to come all the way here to see you. Had you been interested you would have come to see me."

A man must serve three years as an apprentice before he becomes a barber or a plumber, yet some salesmen who have been in the millinery business for years will quit their jobs on a minute's notice to take out a line of hardware if the job promises them twenty dollars a month more.

When you join a club with the thought of having some place to go to spend your lunch hour in rest and relaxation, doesn't it make you madasell to have some fellow member take advantage of a club acquaintance to solicit you for business?

Thank goodness competition in all lines of business has become so keen only men of ability are wanted, and the man with the "pull" is now "the man with the hoe"—or hod.

I never could feel I was in a regular place of business where men called stenographers by their first names.

Don't try to be funny. There is nothing funny about business. It's a serious proposition.

In trying to be as polite as those damphools who take their hats off in department store and office building elevators, I now grab my hat every time a woman gets aboard the street-car in which I am riding.

It isn't what you start that counts—it's what you finish.

When you run across an employee who enjoys the reputation of being a "good fellow," remember Bill Nye's definition of a "good fellow"—a damn fool.

Some salesmen will send in an order for a thousand dollars' worth of merchandise from a man they would not personally trust for nine dollars, and then write a letter roasting the credit man for turning it down. Ain't it the truth?

No organization is complete without a grouch and an air-castle builder.

Seeing is not always believing—I've seen a lot of people I wouldn't believe.

Don't tell your customers what the market is going to be next Fall. If you really know, cash in on that knowledge yourself.

Some employees waste a week's time telling us where they will spend their vacation and then use up another week telling us what they did.

You never hear a busy man complaining about his lot in life. It's always the loafer who does the kicking.

The boss may not be much for literature but he never tires of reading—"Enclosed find orders for—"

Don't waste time telling stories to customers. If you are sure you are a good story teller, try out as a professional entertainer.

There are more real opportunities today than there are real men. P. S. Do you get that?

Don't overlook the clerk of today; from his ranks come the merchants of tomorrow.

A salesman once said to me, "Next week I go north with my line." I am not sure whether he said "line" or "lying."

By the time a prospect gets through deciphering the lodge buttons, pin, charm and monogram rings some salesmen wear, they haven't time enough left to consider his business.

No employee has ever become so valuable to an organization but that there is a better man to take his place. P. S. — It might be a good idea for you to read that one over again.

It does not take the boss long to declare "War" when he sees his employees "soldiering."

When you "talk" a man into buying something, someone else is pretty sure to come along and "talk" him into being dissatisfied with it.

Take my tip and stay off of the continuous job hunter with a pocketful of "To whom it may concern" letters. As Rube Goldberg would say, "they don't mean anything."

Never apologize for calling by saying, "I was just passing and thought I would drop in." Better you tell the prospect you have come quite a bit out of your way to see him.

As the boss entered his office one morning the chief clerk greeted him with the usual "How are you," and he answered "rotten." The sales manager asked the chief clerk how he was feeling, and he replied "rotten." As the salesmen showed up for work and greeted the sales manager with the usual "How are you this morning?" he grunted "rotten." All the salesmen went out to work feeling rotten, and the sales for that day were just as the boss felt—-rotten.

An employee that has the interest of his employer at heart doesn't have to carry a rabbit's foot for luck.

To the fellow who shows up late, and sneaks home early, we are indebted for the "punch clock" system.

"Never explain. Your friends don't require it, and your enemies won't believe you anyway."

Plan ahead. Know today what you are going to do tomorrow—and do it.

Always leave them smiling when you say "goodby."

If that which you have been employed to sell were easy to sell the boss would have hired a man for the job at half the money he is paying you. So be thankful that that which you are selling is hard to sell, and prove to your employer he used good judgment in picking you for a man's job.

Many a man uses up so much of a company's time in thinking he is entitled to an increase in salary that he doesn't have time enough left to earn what he is getting.

It isn't so much the fifteen minutes you show up late, or start home early, that counts, it's the demoralizing effect it has upon the whole organization.

Don't promise delivery in two weeks—it may take four, and buyers have a way of remembering such things against you.

Poker players always tell of their winnings, but make no mention of their losses. Just so it is with a lot of salesmen, who boast of one order they got out of a town, but have nothing to say of the nine they didn't get.

One of the first yelps that comes from a failure who is on his way out is, "They wouldn't give me a show." Nobody gave Barnum a show, but he had the biggest on earth.

Sit still, don't move around. Nervousness is contagious.

The surest, quickest and best way to disrupt an organization is to put a few personal friends and relatives on the payroll.

Simply because a fellow listens to your troubles is no indication that he is interested in them.

I know employees who have "enjoyed" poor health all their lives.

The fellow who drives down to work every morning in a swell car, then goes in and puts up a plea to the boss that because of the high cost of living he should have an increase in salary, has a helluva fine chance getting it.

He who has to depend upon his friends to find him a job is not much of a salesman. If he cannot sell his own services I doubt his ability to sell anything else.

If, in the middle of your solicitation, the prospect is called away, or has a long business talk over the phone, you had just as well be on your way.

The open-face envelopes, which you see coming in for employees the first of each month, do not contain savings bank accounts.

"Go to a friend for advice, a stranger for charity, and a relative for nothing" is a little piece of advice an "old timer" gave me years ago.

Never try to smoke a prospect out with tobacco.

The most detestable cuss around a place of business is the confidential speakeasy scandal-buzzer.

If letter writing and telephoning would bring in orders and signed contracts, you would not be on the payroll as a salesman. Do you get the idea?

A number of business colleges are advertising they teach the "touch system." I have met a number of their graduates.

Never say I "put over," "landed," or "hooked" a prospect. Feel that you are doing more for him in taking his contract than he is doing for you by signing it.

Another splendid way to keep a nervous man's mind off your business while you explain it is to have a few silver dollars in your pocket and jingle them while you talk.

Since the contract, or order, tells all the buyer is to get, there is nothing left for you to promise.

No one thing in life makes a greater coward of a man than debts.

Do what you have to do and do it now. Spell "now" backwards and you have the answer.

Waiting to see small calibre men with little or no authority, has caused many a salesman to have to send his pants to a tailor to be half-soled.

The benches in the parks are filled with fellows who tried to tell the boss how to run his business.

Leave them remembering what you said and not what you wore.

Don't bore your friends by talking business to them. Know your business so well your talk will be interesting.

Nobody expects you to be the man your mother thinks you are, but your employer has a perfect right to expect you to be the man you told him you were.

Laughter—not sighs—scares troubles away.
The loudest barkers are always with the side show.

The first employee the fool killer should brain is the conceited ass who thinks it is his personal popularity that is making it possible for his firm to remain in business.

There is just as much difference between a solicitor and a salesman as there is between a fiddler and a violinist.

Always have a "good-by" check ready for the fellow who can't be told anything.

A lot of employees already have their next summer's vacation plans all worked out in detail, but they haven't the least idea in the world what they are going to do tomorrow.

One time I saw some children playing with a rubber ball. I noticed the harder the ball was thrown down the harder it came back. P. S.—Read that over again.

You never have any trouble in getting in to see a real big business man. Another reason why he is a Big Business Man.

Show a man you are interested in his business and he will become interested in yours.

When you hear a fellow speaking ill of his former employer you don't have to guess as to whether he quit or got fired.

When you have taken an order—the goods have been shipped—received—paid for—the customer is satisfied—and wants more—then—you have made a sale.

Take it from me, there are just as many men on the average payroll who are overpaid as there are those who are underpaid.

The less you listen, the less you learn.

It's worth going broke in business, or losing your job once or twice in life just to find out how many real friends you have.

When you abuse the confidence your employer has in you, your credit and your friends—you are a bum.

Hold your temper and you will hold your friends, and your job.

A college education is supposed to fit you for a position—not entitle you to one.

Of course you may logically prove to yourself that you cannot do as much this year as you did last. I have done it, but logic is a mighty dangerous thing to rely on. I heard of a perfectly logical little girl, but her conclusions were wrong. Her teacher asked her what a furlough was, and she said it was a mule. On inquiry it was found out that the girl had seen a picture of a soldier riding on a mule, and under the picture was the label, "Off on a furlough." The little girl was logical.

If there be any truth in the old saying "some men are born salesmen," then it is indeed too bad such splendid advice as "Ye must be born again" appears in a book so many would-be salesmen seldom read.

Remember "Thoughts are Things."

Stop worrying. Look out for your company's interest. Listen to the advice of your superiors, and you'll get along all right in the business world.

Walt Mason says, "Tho' days be dark and trade be tough, it's always well to make a bluff; to face the world with cheerful eye, as tho' the goose were hanging high."

The fellow that burns midnight oil reading a worthwhile book will have a better tomorrow than the young man burning midnight gasoline to a road-house party.

It's well to have a good opinion of yourself, but it is not advisable to air that opinion too much—it might make you unpopular.

A real friend is he who reminds you of your faults, while your one worst enemy is the man who tells you only those things that please, and makes a fool of you.

Had I the printing of all applications to be filled out by salesmen seeking positions, I would start with these questions: "Are you happy in your home?" "Does your wife take an interest in your work?" I have never known a man to make a success in sales where things were not as they should be at home.

Have you ever noticed how you learn to like the fellow you have done a friendly turn, and how your hate grows for the one you have injured?

The little granddaughter of an old war veteran, after having heard one of his often repeated war stories, said, "Grandpa, didn't anybody at all help you win the war?" I am often reminded of this little story when I meet one of these "I" salesmen, and wonder if there is anybody else in the firm besides him.

Look upon every fellow woman worker as being a lady and every man as a gentleman until they prove themselves to be otherwise.

A shallow talker seldom makes a deep impression.

It is good to keep your muscles in trim by using them, likewise your brain. Much leg work and little head work seldom adds to a salesman's salary.

Happiness is one thing you don't have to go around looking for. If you are entitled to it it will come to you.

A salesman has no need for trick approaches or tricky methods if his goods are right and he is half right.

If there is any question as to what is fair—give the other fellow the advantage.

When I meet one of these inquisitive fellows, I am reminded of the old dog that was moving her family across a railroad track. One inquisitive pup stopped to stick his nose against the third rail. While he found out all there was to know about electricity, it never did him much good.

The old-time "good fellow" salesman whose coming to town was always announced a week ahead with a funny postal card, is having hard sledding since Uncle Sam took the ale out of sale.

Walk straight up to Trouble, look it in the eye and tell it to go to Helena.

A Detroit automobile man writes: "'Take It From Me' has missed but one man, and he is the crazy nut who uses expensive stationery, catalogues, desk blotters, or the telephone book for scribbling while phoning." P. S.—The book is now complete.

Someone has said—"He has achieved success who has lived well, laughed often and loved much; who has gained the trust of pure women and the love of little children. Who has filled his niche in life and accomplished his task; who has left the world better than he found it, whether by an improved poppy, a beautiful poem, or rescued a soul. Who has looked for the best in others, and given the best he had; whose life was an inspiration; whose memory is a benediction. This constitutes success."

2 Listen To This

These little Truths may remind you
of some of your friends—
Likewise, remind them of you

I am a great believer in luck. The harder I work, the more of it I seem to have.

The best way to sell yourself to the boss is by selling that which he has to sell to someone else.

I never had a man whisper anything to me that was worth listening to.

As soon as salaried people find out they can't live Pierce Arrow lives on "Tin Lizzy" salaries, "times" and "conditions" will be all right.

Self starters are about the only automobiles that are in demand. Same may be said about employees.

The fellow who tries to beat a railroad train over a crossing gets where he is going some years ahead of the rest of us, but I am not in any such hurry to "get where I am going."

If you happen to know of a fellow who is waiting for an opportunity you can tell him he need not wait any longer—another fellow went after it and grabbed it.

Keeping busy at the right thing keeps you from doing the wrong thing.

Don't tell people your troubles. L's-fire, they've got plenty of their own.

I always feel like shooting the after-dinner speaker who gets up and starts reading a speech. If he can't remember it, how can he expect others to do so? If no one can remember the fool thing, what's the use of bothering with it?

Say it with kindness while he is living. Don't wait to "say it with flowers" after he's dead.

Do your personal friends ever call you over the 'phone during business hours, right when you are the busiest, and talk 'n, talk 'n talk about nothing? So do mine. 'N I wish mine in the same place you wish yours.

A cat will lie before a fire—men afterwards.

Be sure you know what you are talking about. You know, I have always felt every minister should have been a dawgone good sinner for at least ten years before starting out to preach against sin.

There is a difference between boasting and boosting. One is personal.

Telegraph and taxi companies have the right idea. They do not wait for business to come to them—they go after it.

"I'll tell the world" is a conversational filler used now-a-days by fellows who can't tell anybody anything.

Golf clubs are all right if you can use them. Some people think the same thing about friends.

Constructive thinking and worthwhile suggestions will get you further than "Yesing" and "playing up" to the boss.

Have your boss swear by you—not at you.

Some men never hit the mark because they never pull the trigger.

Make up your mind to beat it, or "beat it."

Look trouble in the face and laugh at it.—P. S. Forget this advice in case your wife or boss happens to be your trouble.

Many a man you meet on the street who says, "I'm going to work"—lies.

You can guess pretty close to what is in a man's head by the clothes he has on his back.

The best way to get to the top is to push the other fellow up ahead, and he will help you stay there.

Never greet a friend with "How are you this morning?" Nine men out of ten look upon such a greeting as a request for a recital of troubles and immediately proceed to unload them.

When the average man dies, he leaves his wealth to his relatives and his troubles to his friends. That is to say, he names his best business friends as executors of his estate. He "wishes" trouble aplenty on men he would in life not have asked for two hours' time. It's all wrong. There are plenty of Trust Companies whose business it is to handle these matters.

Suppose you were your employer, would you keep a man on the payroll at the salary you are getting for the work you are doing?

Looking for faults, like charity, should begin at home.

Loud dress and loud talk have caused many a salesman's solicitation to go unheard.

You are going to get what's coming to you. Doctors may delay it, and ministers may soothe you, but you can't escape it.

More than thirty years ago, I heard Col. P. Watt Hardin say in a political speech down in Kentucky, "I'm for my country against any country, my state against any state in my country, my county against any county in my state, my town against any other town in my county, my street against any other street in my town, and for my side of the street against the other side." If you don't feel just that way about the firm you are with—get out.

When two men form a partnership just because of personal friendship or some relationship, one of the other soon feels he is bearing all the hardship and the business soon goes into the hands of a receivership.

We can't have an ideal national life unless we as individuals have less high life and more home life.

A common expression among salesmen these days is "I'm in the real estate, advertising or life insurance game." Since "Game" suggests "gamble" or "chance" and it is not every man who likes to look upon his insurance policy or real estate buy as being a "chance," I don't know but what it might be just as well to use the word "business," instead of "game."

I could never see the sense of some concerns paying out good money in salaries to high class men when the only set of brains used are those of the boss.

Your tomorrow is going to be what your today makes it.

Daniel Boone made his way through Kentucky when it was a wilderness. Clark drove an ox team to the Pacific and Perry reached the North Pole without the aid of road maps or signboards, but when you start some salesmen out after business, they want to know the name and address of the prospect, man to see, how to get in to see him, what to say and how to say it. Then all they bring back is a "not interested" report.

For your own good, get it out of your fool head this world owes you a living.

Before you have a car of your own you wonder why your friends don't come around and take you for a ride. When you get a car, your friends think the same thing about you.

Every employer is looking for men who see how a thing can be done and then do it.

About the best women workers around any place of business are those you would think the wife of the boss employed.

A Sales Manager was saying to me it was next to impossible to tell a salesman. Your durn tooten it is. Can't tell some of them anything.

Another thing I thank the good Lord for doing is, fixing it so money won't buy happiness. I'm now enjoying at least a million dollars worth a day, and it would be pretty hard to get used to using but seventy-five cents worth.

Don't apologize for what you sell, or the price placed on it; that's just an admission that you think it's wrong.

Many a man politely agrees with you when he don't believe a cussed word you're saying.

Be patient with a fool—that others may be more patient with you.

Think more, earn more, and get more out of life.

Too much celebrating has kept many a man from becoming celebrated.

Take the "ice" out of Service.

No salesman ever won much by winning an argument.

One time up in the mountains of Kentucky a traveler met a mountaineer driving some razor back hogs down the road and stopped to ask him where he was taking them. The old fellow said he was taking them down in the lowlands to turn them out to fatten. The traveler said, "Why, my good man, down in my country we pen our hogs up, and they fatten in so much less time." The old mountaineer thought it over in deep silence for a minute or two and replied, "What the hell's time to a `hawg?" I am often reminded of that story when some "nothing to do" friend calls on me during business hours.

Many a man applies for position fearing he won't get it. If he does, he is afraid he can't hold it. He goes out for business fearing he won't find it. He imparts fear to those he calls upon, until they are afraid to do business with him. The Sales Manager's fear that he has picked a lemon is confirmed and the cashier writes the goodbye check.

Women continue to attend bargain sales, and men keep on buying oil stock, but the question of getting "something for nothing" remains unanswered.

If you are not a success where you are, changing towns or jobs will be of little profit to you until you change your mental attitude.
A little perspiration will help along your inspiration.

Worry breaks up more men than work breaks down.

Now I know why the Standard Oil Company is such a wonderful organization. They tell me that every time an official retires or dies they hire a new office boy.

Suppose Jones and Brown were to form a partnership and go into business. That Jones was on the job from early morning until evening. Brown sleeps away a good part of the morning, enjoys a late breakfast, possibly a morning drive, lunches with friends, perhaps goes to a matinee, then shopping, and spends the day's profits. How long do you think such a partnership would last? Team work alone will win in any partnership. I have always looked upon marriage as being a sort of a partnership affair. Do you get the idea?

If you haven't foresight enough to lay in your winter's fuel during the summer months, it will be just as well not to growl about the price charged for winter delivery.

There are too many salesmen who can't tell a prospect from a suspect.

Never dispute the woman who says she has a model husband. Webster says a model is a small imitation of the real thing.

Let the other fellow talk occasionally—you can't learn much listening to yourself.

Were you ever on a train that had taken the sidetrack for another to pass? As you looked out the window at the other train going by, you felt as though you too were going, but a glance around proved you were standing still. Now, call to mind your competitors, or your fellow employees. — Are you going ahead, or do you just think you are?

The sheriff puts many a salaried man on his feet — by taking away his car.

I encountered a barber a few days ago who knew plenty about the cause of strikes and the politics of the world, but he knew mighty little about barbering. I'm not going there again.

Some people have an idea that to prove themselves optimists they must go around grinning like idiots.

Nice things said to you often cause you to become satisfied with yourself and whenever you get to the point where you think you have reached the degree of perfection, and your employer is too blind to see it, take it from me, boy, you're backing up—and, out.

Our friends make us—we break ourselves.

Love at first sight may be all right, but my advice is, to take a second look before calling a minister.

Some employees will loaf on their jobs all day, then go home and want to lick the corner grocer for "short weighting" them on a dime's worth of potatoes. Aint it the truth?

Treat a dog with kindness, pet him a little, feed him well and he will never leave you.—P. S. This system often works on husbands.

Every time I see a "Buy a Home" advertisement, the thought comes to me—it can't be done. You can buy a house, but a home you must make. Someone has said, a home is a roof over a good woman.

San Francisco is noted for its hilly streets. One morning as I was coming to my office on a Sutter street car, and like most men silently thinking, and worrying about certain problems I was to face during the day, I looked ahead at the high hills our car was going to have to climb, and I wondered how power enough could be generated to push it over the tops of them. As we came to them, it seemed as though they had disappeared, and we were traveling on level ground. That evening as I rode home, I tried to call to mind some of the worries I carried down with me that morning but they, like the hills, had disappeared as I came to them.

Light in and do what you are paid to do, or light out and find something else to do.

The world is not going to charge you with your failures until you quit trying.

Some traveling men get homesick when away from home—others at home.

The trouble is, too many employees just think they think.

The salesman who always offers some concession makes a confession his goods won't sell, or he can't.

The young man who marries a "Cosmetic Jane," lives in a one room apartment over a convenient delicatessen shop, and is making monthly payments on a tinliz, finds it harder to live on his salary than does the husband of "Sunbonnet Sue," who has a modest little home, a garden, flowers and a happy youngster or two.

Some men let not their left hand know their right one has written a check to help out a hungry family, but they generally see that the newspaper finds out all about it.

The most dangerous time of your life has come when you begin to take yourself seriously.

A rolling stone may gather no moss, but the stone that has gathered no moss had better keep rolling.

It's easy to pick out the men as they show up for work in the morning who have had a breakfast table scrap with their wives over the morning paper.—And the profitable thing to do is to let them go back home and scrap it out.

You never hear those who have money in banks speak of cashiers as being "marble hearted tight wads." It's always the fellow who's got nothing, and wants something on a note that's worth nothing who does the "kicking."

You're going to have to do a lot more good than bad, because it's the bad that is mostly remembered.

Have you ever gone to bed wishing it was morning and you were ready to get back on the job? You haven't! Then you do not love your work, and you'll never succeed until you do.

Hold up your head—Look ahead—Go ahead and, get ahead.

The fellow who does just enough to get by, never earns enough to buy much.

The fellow who knows most, says nothing, and lets the man who knows nothing do the talking.

What are you going to do tomorrow?

You can always tell by the service a hotel employee renders you how much longer he is to continue using the tradesman's entrance in coming to work.

Nearly all the heads of big city firms are from small towns. The fear of "I told you so" has put them where they are. When they left the old home town every "old timer" told them of the mistake they were making, that they would soon be back, sad and sorry. Rather than go back a failure to hear the "I told you so" chorus, they worked like sons-of-guns to make good—and, they did.— I know what I am talking about. To no other one thing do I owe more for whatever success I have had, than the fear of "I told you so."

When you give a man a title, give him the authority that goes with it.

Keep moving on the job; there are lots of fellows below you that want to come up. If you don't go ahead they'll go around you.

You can't borrow anything on what you think you are. It's the value others place on you that counts.

It's the idle mind that worries.

Sticktoativeness. That's what you must have if you expect to get anywhere in business.

One day Thompson Dunegan, who was quite a character in my home town, dashed into the office of Judge W. H. McBrayer, and attempted to give the Judge the "rush act" for twenty dollars. The Judge's answer to Thompson's plea was "I have long since discontinued the making of permanent investments." Whenever an oil stock, mining stock or any other sort of a "sure thing" ten to one hundred percent paying stock salesman calls, I make use of the Judge's words of wisdom.

Every man is a salesman, but that does not mean every man can sell everything.

When you think an unkind thing about someone, think several times before you say it.

Men used to get drunk on whiskey, which was pretty bad, but I saw a fellow a day or two ago who was drunk on authority, and it wasn't so much different!

You are paid for doing what you are expected to do. Increases come from doing more than is expected of you.

Never knock a competitor. Next week may find you at his door asking for employment.

The business world is looking for the man who can wrap System in Simplicity and tie it up with something other than red tape.

Scientists tell us the chief difference between man and the animals is that man thinks and the animals do not. Wouldn't it be more accurate to say, some men are capable of being trained to think?

Selfishness in one form or another is responsible for just about all that is not right in this world.

I have met thousands of men who enjoy the satisfaction of knowing they were first in line when brains were being distributed.

Teach your boy how to spend money. When he knows how to buy a hundred cents worth for a dollar, you need not worry about his saving. Again, if he doesn't know how to spend it, what's the use of saving.

Nearly every employer remembers what Sis Hopkins said about "there ain't nothing in doin' nothin' for nobody that ain't doin' nothin' for you." That is why a lot of employee's salaries are never increased.

If men took as good care of themselves as they do of their automobiles this would be a generation of athletes.

In Emerson's day the world might have beaten a path to the door of the man who made the best mousetrap, but to-day it takes advertising enough to convince the people it is the best, with street and house number given, and mention made of parking space for cars while the trap is being examined.

Ships rarely fail to reach the places they start for, but their captains generally know where they are going.

Many years ago, a fellow called my stepfather a liar. I grabbed a pitchfork and was in the act of puncturing him, when my stepfather seized the pitchfork, threw it aside and said, "What are you trying to do? He has but expressed his opinion, and his opinion is not worth anything." Remembering this incident, and weighing the value of personal opinion, I have gone through life having fewer fights.

Truth wins and that's the truth.

Suppose the dog were to succeed in catching the railroad train, he wouldn't know what to do with it. It is quite possible your employer has not seriously considered you for the position you think you are entitled to for the same good reason.

You've got to be a straight shooter if you expect to hit the mark.

It's often the truck a fellow drinks that causes the limousine accident.

You are not through work when you have done that you were told to do, but when all is done there was to do.

The "echo" you hear when "knocking" a competitor is the sound of nails being driven into your own coffin.

Pretty soon the 1:30 A. M. Radio will broadcast, "Has anybody seen my husband?"

It's too durn bad that men are not what their wives and photographers make them out to be.

A New York man refused to buy my book "Take It From Me" for his employees because ten of the 248 paragraphs did not appeal to HIM. I am wondering if there is a man on earth who can say 248 things that would please any one person.

So long as you are well dressed, carry your head up, walk erect and fast, wear a pleasant smile, choose well your associates and don't talk too durn much, the world will invoice you at all you are worth.

When you get an order without an effort it is always a good idea to consult Mr. Dun or Mr. Bradstreet before making shipment.

Put smiles in your letters and in your voice when phoning, then cover your face with one.

The fellow that turns over in bed when the alarm goes off and sleeps away the thirty minutes he should make use of in refreshing himself with a bath, a shave, shoe shine, should for the good of his firm permanently remain in bed.

Musicians, singers and vaudeville performers hold back their best for the "come back" but, the average salesman is not so wise.

Stop, look and listen when you come to a railroad track, but quit doing it when you come to work.

Every responsibility is an opportunity.

Never accept favors you can't return. If your income will not permit your lunching at the better cafes, then do not accept invitations from others to lunch in such places. Do not become a moocher. I know a young man who had a wonderful opportunity with a big concern until he became a "lunch moocher" and ruined himself.

A real boss is a man it's hard to tell from the fellows that are working for him.

Nearly every salesman in "making a town," goes first to the easiest man of all to sell, then the next easiest, etc., leaving the "hard-nuts-to-crack" for the last. As a result, they leave town wearing a grouch that often costs them the business of the "easiest man to sell" in the next town. If they would but reverse things they would wear a smile out of every town and be in a better frame of mind to sell the "hard customers" in the next.

I hate to have some people give me their advice, when I know how bad they need it.

When you have learned how to be friendly with your employees without having them become familiar with you—you're a real boss.

Men who have any considerable amount of money never have much to say about it. Same rule applies to those having religion.

When I see stenographers and switchboard operators on their way to work with library books and sewing baskets, I can better understand why Central gives the signal, "they don't answer."

Do what is to be done, whether it be in your particular department or not. Your success and salary depends entirely upon the success and profits of the firm.

There are too dawgone many men who think that their praying to God on Sunday forgives them for preying upon their fellow men the rest of the week.

While figuring you are entitled to a larger salary than you are getting it is well to remember that figures often lie.

Knock the "'t" off of can't.

If you think it is right to do a thing, why go ahead and do it without asking so many questions. A fellow asked a porter on a train if he could smoke in the car. Displaying much authority the porter answered, "No, sir—I'll say you can't." Looking around, he noticed some other men smoking and he asked, "Well, why is it those men are smoking?" The porter answered, "Coz they didn't ask me—that's why."

Never cuss a hundred dollar a month man for not doing a thing just as you would have done it. If he knew as much as you, you might be working for him.

When I see a poor boob leaving a good job to go in business for himself on a "shoestring," I can't help but shed a sympathetic tear.

Before you go to work in the morning, look yourself over carefully that you may not be overlooked by those who are to look you over all day.

Why not attach alimony coupons to marriage licenses and do away with tiresome court proceedings?

Go into Executive Session with yourself every day. It will do you good.

If you must say "whats-the-use," get your hat and say it to the cashier on your way out.

Ten minutes spent in a barber shop listening to men tell barbers just how to shape their hair and comb it, will convince you there is no such a thing as a "fussy old maid."

Somehow I always thought mighty well of that little piece of Western philosophy "live every day so you can look any damn man in the eye and tell him to go to hell."

If you want to find the best story teller and conversationalist in any office, look for the fellow behind the desk that is piled the highest with unfinished work.

When you hear of a woman being jealous of her husband's stenographer, perhaps you'll find she was his stenographer when he made the discovery his first wife "did not understand him."

You are what others tell others you are, and your business is just what others tell others it is.—P. S. Read that one again.

If you are out of a position, it is your personal appearance that is going to have much to do with your securing one. And, just as much to do with your holding it. Dress well, it pays.

When you have passed Selfishness, Untruthfulness, Jealousy and Egotism, then Success is the next station.

Have you ever noticed how much more money some fellows will give to charity when they can stand up before a crowd and yell out the amount than when the appeal comes to them by mail and there is nobody around but God and them when the amount is filled in? And they take a chance God is not looking.

What you once were does not interest your employer one bit. It's what you are today, and what you're going to be tomorrow that counts.

When you go to bat make up your mind you are going to make a home run, not a bunt. Be a "home run" salesman, not a "bunting" order taker. Some salesmen try to make a thirty minute solicitation in five minutes, and some merchants pile a little of everything they have in stock in a show window. As a result the buyer is so confused the sale is lost.

Quit grouching around. If you are not satisfied with your job, quit.

The fellow you hear complaining to everyone around the office about not getting an increase, knows durn well he would get fired for not earning what he is getting were he to say anything to his employer.

Now that it's all over, what did you really do yesterday that's worth mentioning.

When a fellow runs across the street, stumbles, falls in front of a car and is killed, the evidence at the inquest usually shows it made durn little difference which side of the street he was on.

If a salesman could only make the arguments to prospects during the day he thinks of at night after he has gone to bed—Eh!

Life insurance is the salaried man's one best bet. Don't figure how little you can carry but, how much.

Of course it is easy for you to see how your boss could double the business by using your judgment in the place of his own, but he has likely taken into consideration the fact you have had the exclusive use of your judgment all your life, and it's got you nothing.

"You can't buy confidence and respect with profanity and vulgarity," says Coleman Cox in "Take It From Me." He ought to say this in the smoking compartments of Pullman cars. (Rotary-grams, Beaumont, Texas.) A dawgone good suggestion.

The man who does not want to find out the facts does not want the facts found out.

The fellow who makes his own way, generally has his own way.

A firm whose store front has not been painted since the building was erected will spend thousands of dollars a year to have their name painted on "dead walls" in the city, and barns in the country. Their delivery trucks that are seen by thousands and thousands of people every day, as they travel the streets, are never painted from the time they are built until the junk man gets them.

Do you remember the old time traveling salesman whose side-line used to be "here's a good one I heard the other day." I haven't seen one of those fellows since the Eighteenth Amendment became operative.

The more a man concentrates on his own business the less he knows about the other fellow's business. If I wanted to buy oil or mining stock at a bargain I would call on our most successful attorneys and doctors.

A young man came in to see me the other day and said he was looking for a position. I admired his honesty. Most of them say they are looking for work.

An interesting talker is one who talks about something the other fellow is interested in.

Don't grin—smile.

No corporation has ever grown to be big enough, and no labor organization has ever become strong enough to succeed without the good-will of the people.

As an employee I never asked for a testimonial letter, and I have always declined to read those offered me by men seeking positions. Some one was telling me about an employer who was asked by a man he had just discharged for a letter of recommendation. Turning to his stenographer he dictated the following:—"The bearer has worked for me one week, and I am satisfied that is long enough."

When you do your work better than anyone else has ever done it, you will hold your job longer than anyone else.

We may have another war sometime and if we do I want the front ranks made up of the fellows who greet me with the stereotyped "wha-diy'kno."

You have likely met the man who has nice things to say to everyone except at home, and who is polite to all women except his wife. You know the fellow I mean. The one who gets in an elevator with his wife and keeps his hat on until some painted dame gets in.

Habit is a great thing if properly directed. Politeness, gentleness, honesty and veracity may be our habits if we will practise these virtues long enough.

A boy who from his earliest remembrance has been told that he will be whipped when his father returns from work is not very likely to become chummy with his dad.

Don't complain because everyone does not agree with you. After having used a dictaphone for a number of years I am surprised when I try to pen a letter to see how much Mr. Webster and I differ on spelling.

When you repeat that which someone has told you, knowing it to be untrue, the Recording Angel charges you up with another lie.

A fellow rode into a little mountain town down in Kentucky and made it known that he was looking for trouble. The verdict of the coroner's jury read "Plain case of suicide."

I met a young man sometime ago who was telling me how little his manager knew about running the business. I saw him again yesterday and he told me he had "resigned" his position.

The big advertisements some concerns run every day offering their merchandise at cost of course attract my attention, and they quite often create in me a desire for some of the advertised articles. When they do I usually go to some store I have confidence in and make my purchases.

I suppose it is just as well the newspapers only print the names of those "held up" by footpads, and not those that are being held up by friends and relatives.

Did you ever have one of those "lead pencil fortune makers" come to you with a scheme to make a lot of money out of a business he is engaged in. The plot usually calls for its being made out of some other fellow's business—about which he knows nothing.

In naming a product you expect to advertise it is well to select some name that offers a suggestion. As example: "Uneeda Biscuit" or "Dodge Automobiles."

Anyone can tell you something you don't know. Ask questions—then listen.

I could tell those younger in sales than I, hundreds of tricks and schemes I have used in getting in to see buyers, but none of them ever got me any business.

"Staying with it" has often brought success to men not overly burdened with the qualifications we like to think successful men should have.

Every woman should take a vacation each year away from her family. By her absence her family will measure her full worth.

The difference in value between a kicking man and a kicking mule is not very much—and neither one is an asset to any business.

There is no substitute for Truth.

An incompetent man who through influence or favor has landed a good paying position which he can't fill, is about as well off as the man who had the bear by the tail.

We frequently try to blame the National Administration, the tariff or the late war for a condition of affairs which down in our heart we know devilish well was brought about by ourselves.

Just about the busiest thing in the world is a hen scratching for one chick. We must give the hen credit for not letting up on her energy because the chick crop was not what she expected.

Write every business letter as though it were a telegram and you were to pay for the sending of it.

Don't close your eyes tonight until you can call to mind some good you have done today.

The advice of men who have made fortunes is worth more to you than that of those who tell fortunes.

More money—more money! Not that they have any need of it, but to possess it, do we see men giving up those things money can't buy. As Puck says, "What fools these mortals be."

Bachelors are said to be more conceited than married men. Should you be interested in knowing why such is true I would advise your "listening in" on a bridge party some evening when a dozen ninety pound wives are reducing their two hundred pound husbands to boys' size.

Too many men looking for work quit looking for it when they find jobs.

A boy is never convinced that his balloon is as large as he can make it until it bursts. It is too bad he forgets his balloon experience when he grows to be a man and gets into business.

When a prospect says "No," to a salesman's solicitation there's generally a reason—sometimes it is the salesman.

Clothes may not entirely make the man, but they go a long ways toward making first impressions and that counts quite a lot.

3

Just Plain Talk

Editor's note:

This chapter originally appeared as a booklet entitled *Just Plain Talk.* The following is Coleman Cox's original introduction to that booklet:

While I am of course happy to think my little books "Take It From Me" and "Listen to This" have more than likely proved the most successful books of the kind printed in many years, there is something that means far more to me than all the fame or money they could bring, and that is, the Good Friends they have made me in all parts of the world.

It pleases me very much to open this new book with a number of wonderful paragraphs of advice and worthwhile thoughts that have been specially written for it by some of the best known, and most successful men in the world.

No higher compliment could be paid this little book of mine than to make it the message carrier that is to deliver these wonderful truths to you, and to millions of others who will read them with pleasure and profit.

- Coleman Cox

C. M. SCHWAB
Chairman Bethlehem Steel Corporation
New York

If a young man in industry would ask me for advice I would say: "Do not be afraid of impairing your health or giving a few extra hours to the company that pays your salary. Do not be reluctant about putting on overalls. Bare hands grip success better than kid gloves. Be thorough in all things no matter how small or distasteful.

The man who counts his hours and kicks about his salary is a self-elected failure. A man will succeed in anything for which he has real enthusiasm, in which he is genuinely interested, provided that he will take more thought about his job than the men working with him. The fellow who sits still and does what he is told will never be told to do big things.

Captains of industry are not hunting money, they are seeking brains—specialized brains—and faithful, loyal service. Brains are needed to carry out the plans of those who furnish the capital.

To my mind the best investment a young man starting out in business could possibly make is to give all his time, all his energies to work, just plain, hard work."

- C. M. Schwab

EDWARD B. BUTLER
President Butler Brothers
Chicago

Every man is enthusiastic at times. One man has enthusiasm for thirty minutes—another man has it for thirty days, but it is the man who has it for thirty years who makes a success in life.

- Edward B. Butler

WM. B. JOYCE
Chairman
National Surety Company
New York

Here is my favorite formula on success:

(1) Success cannot be purchased.
(2) Success cannot be found.
(3) Success cannot be stolen.
(4) Success cannot be received as a gift.
(5) Success cannot be inherited.

After all there is just one royal road to Success, and it is:

"Do your work in a better way than it has ever been done in the past by anyone, and try and do it better than any one in the future can do it."

- WM. B. Joyce

B. HAL. BROWN
President and General Manager
Prudential Trust Company
Montreal

The Worker--engaged in honest toil, whose ideal is "useful activity;" who believes in the Dignity of Labor—is encouraged by the recorded experience of THE PAST, and utilizes the same in dealing with problems of THE LIVING PRESENT. He develops Character, commands respect, and secures co-operation, assuring steady progress towards the Goal of Unqualified Success and Unenvied Independence.

- B. Hal. Brown

LUTHER BURBANK
Santa Rosa, California

It is well for people who think, to change their minds occasionally in order to keep them clean. For those who do not think it is best at least to rearrange their prejudices once in a while.

Straightforward honesty always pays better dividends than zigzag policy. It gives one individuality, self-respect, and power to take the initiative, saving all the trouble of constant tacking to catch the popular breeze.

Education gives no one any new force, it can only discipline nature's energies to develop in natural and useful directions so that the voyage of life may be a useful and happy one—so that life may not be blasted or completely cut off before thought and experience have ripened into useful fruit.

When the love of truth for truth's sake--this poetic idealism, this intuitive perception, this growth from within—has been awakened and cultivated, thoughts live and are transmitted into endless forms of beauty and utility; but to receive this new growth we must cultivate a sturdy self-respect, we must break away from the mere petrified word-pictures of others and cultivate the "still small voice" within by which we become strong in individual thought and quick in action, not cropped, hedged and distorted by outward, trivial forms, fads and fancies.

- Luther Burbank

HUDSON MAXIM
Hudson Park Landing, New Jersey

Nature rewards usefulness.

Service to others serves the server.

We grow not only on what we feed, but also we grow mentally and physically on what we do; and the bigger the things we do, the bigger we grow.

He who looks to the sky and tries to "hitch his wagon to a star," grows taller toward the stars.

Life is a reaction between the individual and environing stimuli, so that every individual must of necessity develop, both mentally and physically, according as he is acted upon by and reacts to the stimulus of his environment.

Whereas happiness consists in the pleasure derived from the exercise of faculty, the greatest possible asset is that which gives us the most of such exercise—in other words, puts us most to use. An old wife, an old dog and ready money are a man's best friends, and the old wife withal a man's best asset. Loyalty is the noblest of all human attributes, and that kind of loyalty which makes the good wife stand by a fellow through thick and thin, with always unstinted service and sacrifice, in spite of his many littlenesses which she knows all about, clear down to his naked soul—and is too big ever to mention—makes the good old wife a ministering angel to whom one may bow his reverential head.

Believe me, it might be difficult to put more wisdom of good advice into the measure of fifty words, than to quote the following from "The Ruins of Empires," by Count Volney: "All wisdom, all perfection, all law, all virtue, all philosophy, consist in the practice of these axioms founded on our own organization: Preserve thyself; Instruct thyself; Moderate thyself; Live for thy fellow citizens, that they may live for thee."

- Hudson Maxim

COLEMAN DU PONT
Wilmington, Del.

To succeed in life adopt several rules or mottoes.

Always stand without hitching.

Be on your job before the whistle blows.

Don't stop work until you come to a stopping place after the whistle blows.

When you start a job concentrate on it until it is finished well.

When you play, do likewise.

Make few promises; keep them.

If you don't like your job do not blame the boss; it's your fault.

Always be honest. Never tell tales.

Before you do anything, think it over, then think it over again.

Happiness is nowhere in particular; it is a condition.

- Coleman du Pont

E. A. STUART
President Carnation Milk Products Co.
Chicago-Seattle

My observation indicates—if a man is happy in his home he is happy in his work—and happiness is the pathway to success.

When a man takes time to THINK, his vision of material objects and things becomes more valuable to society. When a man thinks, he grows—mentally.

To have a desire to see something grow—to create something new—then help develop it, is valuable to the individual and to the community as a whole.

- E.A. Stuart

CORNELIUS VANDERBILT
New York

Lack of confidence and lack of information sleep in the same bed, locked in the closest kind of embrace. When a man has confidence he gets along in business, but without confidence he might just as well not enter business at all. For confidence is the son of vision, and is sired by information. One of our foremost business executives once told me that it would be a wonderful thing for American industry and for the peace of mind of every business man, if we could replace all rumors with facts. So business, good business, is the substitution of information for guess-work.

- Cornelius Vanderbilt

GEO. S. PARKER
President The Parker Pen Co.
Janesville, Wis.

In each twenty-four hours you use up one of your allotted days. In the use of this day, have you made the best possible use of your talents? Are you, as master craftsmen, building into the pens and pencils you make each day that subtle "something," putting into them the final mystic touch that distinguishes your work from that of a mere time worker?

Are you putting into this work your best thought creations, your ideals, your best—-better than is done by others with less aim and vision?

To such there comes the happiness and the satisfaction of adding to the world's supply of beautiful and useful things.

If so, 'tis enough.

- Geo. S. Parker

WM. H. TAFT
Chief Justice Supreme Court of the United States
Former President

There never was a time in the history of industry and business when men who really work were more quickly noted and more certainly appreciated and advanced. This is because so many young men are looking for soft places, where the pay is good and the work light. They think only of their pay and not what they are to give for that pay. This spirit in itself spoils their work. Work is the greatest boon ever conferred on man. Had he have been able to live without it his development and his civilization would have been hopeless. Work involves resistance to temptation to idleness and pleasure. It trains one in self control. It forms the habit of industry so that the individual craves work as the basis of a happy life. It is a great moral factor. Men differ in their natural qualities, but the application of hard, continuous, intelligent labor, which is within the power of all, levels much of the initial inequalities and gives the palm to the leveler.

All lasting success depends on labor. Genius is the taking of infinite pains. Many a brilliant youth has given promise of greatness. I have known a number—handsome, attractive, facile, and eloquent of speech, acute of intellect. Everything seemed to favor their leadership. Years passed and they did not advance. Young men who had been obscure when they were winning plaudits, have come into prominence and have moved by them. Why? They relied on their natural advantages. They ceased to progress. Labor, hard labor, is necessary to keep up with the needs of the times, with the demands of changing society, with the development of business, of professions, of human activities. The man with the average mentality, but with control, with a definite goal, and a clear perception of how it can be gained, and above all with the power of application and labor, wins in the end.

- WM.H. Taft

Some business partners get along just about as harmoniously as a couple I happen to know. The husband is trying to quit smoking and the wife is dieting to reduce.

There is only one man living who can make a man out of you—that's you.

It is a good idea not to believe more than half you hear, and less than that of what you think.

Profits, not prophets, foretell the future.

When a man "knocks" a town he makes a confession he was a failure in it.

It's not the large payroll, but the small men on it that heads a business for the bow-wows.

Let no man point the finger of scorn at you in years to come because of the way you lived today.

Every day is Judgment Day—use a lot of it.

Don't do so much conversational detouring before arriving at a point of interest.

After this I hope we pay cash for our wars. Just about the time I seem to be cured of cussin' it's time to make up another income tax report.

Another trouble in this world is that fathers are the only visible means of support of too many young men.

I think the time near when all advertisements for female office help and sales ladies will close with "strictly informal."

I was born lucky. All my parents, relatives and friends had to give me was advice.

While some employees are telling what they have done in the past, and are going to do in the future, the boss is looking for someone who can do their work now.

In making collections to pay for a picnic, dance or banquet, it is well to get your money before the music stops playing.

If laundrymen would but carry out the gigantic schemes outlined on restaurant tablecloths they would soon be able to retire from business.

When I was a boy down in old Kentucky the river used to get on a rampage every spring and we would all go down and watch the driftwood on its way. Nobody wanted it—it was only driftwood. Often, in the years that have passed, when men applying to me for positions have named firms by the dozen they had worked for, my mind would go back to Kentucky, and again I would see driftwood, just driftwood, that nobody wants.

I know a fellow who walked the streets for weeks trying to find a job, but was unsuccessful and, what do you suppose he did? Well sir, he opened an employment agency to get jobs for others. I was telling a friend of mine about him, and he laughed and said, "Why 'dogonit, that's nothing. I know a fellow who has been a failure at everything he ever tackled in his life, and sometime ago he announced himself an efficiency expert, and now the largest concerns in the city are paying him big money to tell them how to run their business."

It is hard to guess the income of some employees by the way they spend money, but it's easy enough to guess the outcome.

When a salesman makes a fifteen minute walk to save carfare, because "the house" does not pay such petty expenses, he is placing a value of twenty cents an hour on his time, or a dollar and sixty cents a day. Well, I don't know but what that is a pretty fair estimate of his worth.

Liberality is a thing some men use when out for lunch in buying favorable impressions of waiters and hat checking girls, but their nature changes when the wife wants a few dollars added to her monthly housekeeping allowance.

The salesman who puts in a good part of tonight playing "two bit limit" poker will start tomorrow with a ten percent limit sales ability.

As a rule it's only the conceited who are contented.

A salesman was telling me the human voice was the sweetest thing in the world. I knew whose he meant.

Practice makes perfect. I know a young man who made it a practice of mooching lunches until he is now a perfect dead-beat.

You can't get along without your employer, and he can't get along without you, but he might find it easier to get along without you, than you would find it getting along without him. Do you get the idea?

Regrets generally come so late in life they are of little use. There is but one way to avoid old man Regret and that is to do just as near right as you know how all the time.

I have often heard it said "Everyone has at some time in life contemplated suicide, and murder." Well, I have never given much thought to suicide, because I'm fairly well satisfied here, but I will confess it's pretty hard for me to keep murder notions out of my mind when I see a great big healthy looking young man with a patent leather shine on his hair leading a bunch of half dressed girls in a cabaret review.

Every concern is on the lookout for good men and that is why you seldom hear a good man complaining about not getting enough salary. When the firm he is with fails to pay him all his services are worth some one else is going to come along and do it.

It is always an empty head that swells.

If I had cultivated the savings bank habit in my youth I would have been spared a good many trying hours in my life. Yessir, I would not now be trying to peddle what I've found out during my thirty-three years of active business life for two bits.

I can't see where the inventor of the new "lie detector" machine expects to find a market for the thing for I know of no married man but what has one.

Most all family automobiles are driven by the back axle, and from the back seat.

Some time ago ten thousand and more people cheered a "human fly" as he climbed a New York sky scraper—when his foot slipped—they all turned from him—and but three people attended his funeral. Just so it is with all of us in every walk of life. The world cheers as we climb up, but when our foot slips, and we start down—the cheering stops, and they turn from us. Gee Whiz, there's a wonderful lesson to be learned from that little story if you get it.

Styles come and go but the fellow who sticks to old fashioned morals seems to get along all right.

Mark Twain once said a mine was a hole in the ground owned by a damn liar. Had Mark lived to have bought some oil stock from the same fellow I did he could have said as much of an oil well.

Every concern "takes" stock about once a year. That is, they invoice all merchandise, estimate the value of equipment less depreciation, and charge off, or add so much for increased value of real estate, but how many firms re-estimate the value of their employees, and how many employees "take stock" of themselves. Well, it ought to be done.

Many a man wins a wife with love, attention and consideration, then expects her to be happy and contented with a maid, a cook, and a chauffeur.

The fellow that takes an interest in a business soon owns an interest in it.

It's a wonder to me no one has thought to organize a "Positions Union" in this country. The streets, parks and hotel lobbies are filled with young men of no business experience or ability, who feel themselves eligible to membership in the "Chairman of the Board, President and General Managers" branch of such a Union.

Here's a little piece of confidential advice that's going to be worth a lot to you. Let someone else employ your relatives, personal friends, brother lodge, club and church members.

To some people home is just a place from which you start for picture shows.

Have you ever happened to listen-in when a traveling salesman was trying to pacify one of his pet customers who had just received a letter from the accounting department of his firm saying a check to cover bills past due would be appreciated? So have I. And have you noticed it always turns out that the credit man who wrote the letter is either a young fellow who knows nothing, or an old fossil that nobody pays any attention to.

Never repeat anything told you in confidence, for nine times out of ten it's not true, or is scandal, and the repeating of it is the courting of trouble for you and the other fellow too.

If men could but overlook the faults in others as easily as they excuse their own. By Jimminy, yes.

As we must buy happiness with happiness, just so we must buy better jobs with the jobs we have.

There are times when we all feel we would like to "step on the gas" but it is not always convenient to knock a man down and put a foot in his mouth.

It matters not whose payroll you are on you are working for yourself.

I don't know whether there is any truth in the old adage "Money is the root of all evil" or not, but I have noticed that when a fellow quits "rooting" for money the world quits "rooting" for him.

We are all born honest, truthful, unselfish, free from worry and happy. All of which makes it easier for us to account for so many "self made men."

An ounce of precaution in the form of garlic, and a steak smothered with onions is a bully good feed to give husbands having many important business engagements on for every evening.

When you take a train you are told as to about when you will get where you are starting for. I don't know but what employees would be more efficient and contented if employers would give them some such information when they take a job.

When employing men or women for sales or office work it is well to remember that conservative dressers are conservative thinkers.

Some fellows seem to think that in order to convince me they are my friends they must tell me all their troubles and permanently borrow some of the few dollars I've had to work like the deuce for.
Truth and Honesty are Fear's worst enemies.

I'm a great believer in the power of suggestion. As example, the excuses a salesman sends me, in the place of orders, suggest my getting another man for the job.

Because you have worked hard all day and have another busy day ahead of you tomorrow are no good reasons for your insisting upon your wife taking you window shopping, or over to a neighbors to play bridge.

A fellow asked me why a consignment loaded in a railroad car was called a shipment, and if put aboard a ship it was a cargo. How do I know?

I have always made it a rule to explain to all new salesmen employed that the first thing I read in the morning paper is the weather report and all information regarding business conditions. That I do this to save our salesmen having to bother about sending in such reports, and to give them more time to the writing and sending in of orders.

Never kick about an employee losing his temper. He'll be better off without it.

High flyers seldom light in responsible positions.

I met a salesman some time ago who was telling me, that unless the old man came through with more money he was going with another firm and what he would do to the old concern would be a plenty. It was the first one of these premeditated mercantile murders I have heard since brass foot rails went out of style. Reminded me of a story some fellow was telling about a flea crawling up the hind leg of an elephant with murder in his heart.

The fellow who tells the absolute truth as to his capability and aspirations when applying for a position has little to worry about when he gets it.

I can understand how a rabbit foot in a man's pocket might bring him good luck by his wife mistaking it for a mouse.

Promoters often talk a good deal without giving one.

Believe in God, yourself, your employer, the merchandise you are selling, your associates, then believe in success—for it is yours.

Have you ever noticed the number of married women who think it their sacred duty to "raise" their husbands.

I have known many men who have done right all their lives, yet they've never done any good.

Preaching thrift to a man who carries his small change in a purse is a waste of time.

The man who in leaving home in the morning closes a door behind which is happiness, is pretty sure to open the door to a successful business day.

It is the fellow who studies himself, knows his qualifications and limitations, finds himself a job, sticks to it, and makes a position of it, that succeeds when those looking for positions paying big salaries fail.

The best selling novelty in San Francisco Oriental Stores are the three little Monkeys, one with the paws covering the eyes, the second its ears, the third its mouth. Meaning, see no evil, hear no evil, speak no evil. Every man should have one of these on his desk, and give it two minutes silent thought every morning to insure a more happy and successful day.

The world is waiting to listen when you have something to say—I said something.

Most successful men "blushingly" credit themselves with being "self made" but all failures give full credit to the world at large for their condition.

I have met a number of young fellows who's greatest boast was they "came from good families." A railroad ticket will have to be sent most of them to get back.

A good time to move on, or close your ears is when some reference is made to a successful man, and A Failure opens up with "I knew him when—"

When a salesman "loses his grip" he had just as well send in his sample case to the house.

You are showing symptoms of being under self control if you only talk when you have something to say.

A young lady just out from the East to take a position with a San Francisco firm said "I see the men out here are just as bad as they are in New York about trying to flirt with girls on the street." Another young lady answered "Oh yes, you'll see what you are looking for wherever you go."

The "I'm agin it" man is more often entirely ignorant than part wise. It takes thinking to be for or against anything, and "I'm agin it" is the world's best substitute for thinking.

Quit working for a salary and work for a future.

If you will but take a walk around town, look over those you meet, asking yourself whether or not you would care to change places with them in life, you will become convinced the all wise Maker has been pretty good to you and you haven't sense enough to appreciate it.

All the average girl of today knows about a needle is, that a fiber one is no good for jazz records.

Jumping at a conclusion, like jumping a moving train is dawgon dangerous business.

We had camouflaging long before the war. I have known many employees to kick for an increase to hide the fact they were not earning what they were getting.

A man can't help it because he is tall or short, thick or thin, bald, or has red hair, nor can he help it because his name amuses you, or his taste regarding the clothes he is wearing does not particularly please you. All of these things are of no concern to you, and the less you say about them the fewer people you will offend, and the more friends you are going to have.

Before your self satisfied feeling of importance causes you to lose any sleep worrying about how this old world is going to get along without you, just try to name the Presidents of the United States who are dead.

It is easy enough to tell whether it's a salesman or a collector that is calling. If he is told to come back again, he is more than likely not a salesman.

It's a good policy to carry life insurance, provided it's a good policy.

Some say it costs less to walk than drive a car, but its more comfortable to be in one than under one.

Another way of writing the Golden Rule is "Help a Man to Help Himself."

Many a young man who enters the door of success is "given the gate."

The hardest job of all is that of finding a soft job.

Many years ago I was waiting for a train at a little station up in Northern Michigan, when an old "Lumber Jack" came up, dropped his "turkey," a grain sack in which the "Lumber Jack" carries his wearing apparel and other belongings, upon the platform, turned to me and said, "The accumulation of sixty-two years." Wellsir, do you know that old sack has been haunting me for thirty years. The other night when my wife said to me "Coleman, you will be fifty-one years old tomorrow," the first thought to come to my mind was "and what have I in my sack?"

Today is the day, but that does not mean you should forget the lessons learned yesterday, and not plan well for the coming of tomorrow.

So many salesmen stop thinking when they start talking.

Let the talk of scandal buzzers come in one ear and out the other, and not in one ear and out the mouth.

Nearly all employees give themselves the "benefit of the doubt."

A young fellow applying to me for a position as a salesman said, "I can sell anything." I have seen lots of medicines advertised to cure anything but I never believed in them.

Anyone can be happy by thinking of all they have that should bring happiness.

The popularity of the automobile has not lessened the value of "horse sense" in the least.

When a man says to me "You can't tell me anything" —I believe him.

Concentration, inspiration and application dampened a little with perspiration will help you reach your destination.

Take off your hat to Adversity—then take off your coat, roll up your sleeves and lick it.

"Tomorrow never comes." I've heard that all my life, but I'll be dawgon my catskins if I'm going to bed any night without having my plans for it all worked out.

We usually tell of the faults we see in others because it takes so much less time than it would to tell our own.

We used to have a street car conductor on our line who was always watching for an opportunity to help ladies with children, and old people on and off his car. He was most accommodating to all travelers, called streets, so people could understand him, in fact he ran the car like he owned it and was trying to build up a business. I knew it would only be a course of time until some business man would recognize his worth and give him a better job, and that is what happened

Your sales manager is more interested in knowing just what your plans are for tomorrow than he is in hearing the history of your past life.

What's the use of making the sale if you don't close it.

Money is made on "turn overs" and lost on "hold overs."

Dislikes for others are not always formed because of their faults, but because they have found out something about ours.

Have you ever noticed the young man who went to college usually makes a better business man than the one who was sent to college?

If you "have it in" for someone, better "have it out" with them and quit grouching around.

Ninety-nine men out of a hundred marry because they want the comforts they think a home will give them. Of course, it sounds funny when out in "polite society," to say your husband decided to marry a wife and hire a cook, but you can take it from me, he is going to do more boasting about some good eats fixed for him than he is of your ability to play poker and smoke cigarettes.

Another way to prove yourself "right" with your employer is to confess you are wrong when you know you are not right.

Fearlessness is the mother of confidence.

Some employees seem to think bankers are the only ones whose success depends upon the interest they take in their business.

Traffic officers and not employers are the ones who caution young men against speeding up and trying to go ahead of everyone.

Make people respect you. You can start them doing it by always respecting others.

When a man tells you he is busy as a bee, it's well to remember a bee is his busiest when trying to sting somebody.

The fellow seated just in front of me on a street car was mad because a man in front of him was smoking a pipe. I didn't seem to get much pleasure out of the clouds of smoke from the Egyptian cigarette he was blowing back in my face, and the lady seated back of me didn't like it when I cussed out loud.

An employee that is continually looking for a chance to "get even" with someone never goes ahead of anyone.

Life's darkest moments for a man are those when he is standing in his own light.

I don't know but there is more to be gained by studying those who have failed than in trying to follow in the footsteps of the successful.

When you suspicion your employer suspicions you are not the man you should be, there is usually grounds for suspicion.

When I am asked right quick as to what it takes to make a salesman, I answer "brains and feet."

The best time to get another order is right after you have gotten one.

When contentment enters progress ceases.

I take-in a picture show nearly every night. Yessir, after dinner I'll load up my old pipe, ease into my rocker before the fire, and proceed to run off reel after reel of such pictures as "Boyhood Days," "Friends Here and There" and a few short reels of Current Events of "Yesterday, Today and Tomorrow."

Hard luck is composed of laziness and poor judgment.

The man who can conquer the worst in himself has met and solved the biggest problem he will ever face.

I have never seen the face of a clock that could tell me when to go to work or quit.

When you ask a Sales Manager you are applying to for a position what the salary is to be, and he tells you "the sky is the limit," just take it from me, boy, it's "blue sky" you are going to be expected to sell.

There are two types of men I never care to meet—one is sorry for himself and the other is quite sure there is nothing right in the world.

A crooked path is the shortest way to the penitentiary.

To know how is good, to be able to do is better, but to help others to do is best.

When a certain big shoe manufacturing concern places their line with a dealer they not only sell the clerks, who are to sell the customers, but they take their names and home address, that they may from time to time mail them little sales helps, Christmas, birthday and wedding anniversary remembrances. They well know the success or failure of their business is in the hands of the retail salesmen who come in direct contact with the customer, and they not only make a friend of him, but cultivate and hold his friendship.

Don't always judge a man by the speed at which he travels—the small hand on the clock dial is just as useful as the long one.

When you say your prayers don't ask for anything except that to which you are entitled and for which you are willing to work.

Keeping sober means more than abstaining from the use of bootleg whiskey. It means sane thinking and honest efforts to succeed in a regular rather than the spectacular way.

Men and mules are much alike in that they can often be led where they can't be driven.

The greatest rejuvenation that mankind knows is work of the kind that man likes to do—knows how to do and does in a way that the doer feels he is doing something.

When a man is "all run down" and needs building up he calls in a doctor for advice, and medicine that will put him right. He does not dispute the doctor's diagnosis of his case, or rewrite the prescription to suit himself. How different it is when his business is "run down" and needs building up. He calls in an advertising man whose business it is to stimulate, and build up a run down business. He rewrites the advertising man's "prescriptions" as fast as they are handed to him, changes the size of doses and time of giving to suit himself, and then puts all blame on the advertising man if the business does not show immediate improvement. Yes, the advertising business is the only business in the world every man "knows"—or thinks he knows.

When a man goes to sleep on his job don't wake him, just give the job to someone already awake.

It is pretty hard to help the fellow that makes little or no effort to help himself. I have in mind a man who should go into dry dock and have the human leaches and barnacles that have long been hanging to him scraped off, for his own good, and the good of his friends who he is continually imposing these no good bums upon as men worthy of employment.

Remember the fellow who used to want someone to hold his coat so he could fight. I met him the other day, he was telling everyone he was going to quit his job—everyone except the boss.

A golfer asked me why it is that men who are absolutely honest in business will cheat when playing golf. The only answer I can give is they have not the same chance to be crooked when behind a desk or a counter they have when behind a bunch of trees.

System is a great thing but when an office gets so full of system that it takes two men to keep track of what one is doing, then it's about time to get a new system.

When packing your grip to attend a sales conference it is just as well you leave out your alibis, and imaginary troubles, that no one is at all interested in, and bring along a few new ideas that can be used to an advantage by the other boys.

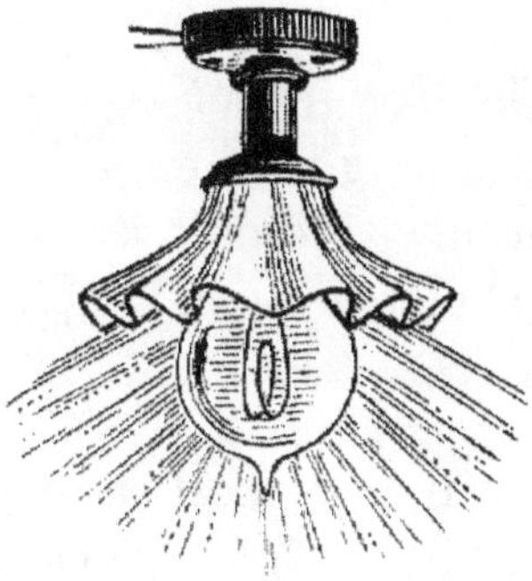

Friends, like promises, when made should be kept.

Before a man erects a skyscraper, or presents his city with a library, park or something of the sort to perpetuate his memory, he should remember that people have a habit of asking "How did he get his money?"

Never lend an ear to the "stool pigeon" who wants to tell you the short comings of other employees. A fellow that will doublecross the men he is working with, will double-cross those he's working for.

Every man is some boy's ideal. Then try and live your life in a way that will make the boy that is trying to imitate you a Real Man.

I know a business man—that is, we are going to call him a business man—who is as fussy as any old maid about his dress, and no representative calling on the trade has a chance of lingering long on his payroll unless he is just as particular about his personal appearance. But, when it comes to writing letters, or getting up sales letters to the trade, the cheapest doggone stationery money can buy is used, and all good impressions are knocked into a cocked hat. Letters are our representatives and we can't dress them too well.

After having lived the greater part of my fifty-two years in the hotels of many states I am thoroughly convinced that the greatest kickers are those who at home are not accustomed to anything like the service and comforts they complain about.

The Credit Men of the country tried out the "Say it with Flowers" idea long before the florists ever thought of it, but for some reason or other it didn't seem to work in all cases, and they had to go back to "please remit."

The time of most employers is so taken up during business hours they usually consider changes, promotions and salary increases either before the business of the day starts, or after hours. I have noticed that the fellow who gets around early, and stays as late as is necessary to finish up the day's work usually gets the promotion and increase in salary.

When you own your own home you enjoy a certain amount of self respect no renter ever knows. Your credit is unquestioned. You are looked upon as being a reliable, trustworthy citizen, and not a floater. Employers want just such independent men on their payroll. The man who owns his own home is a Mr. Somebody in his town.

Many a man that removes his hat when entering an elevator with his wife is credited with being gallant, when he's nothing more than well trained.

You must have sand if you expect to make the grade.

When Alibi Ike gets word his Sales Manager is to visit him, he immediately lists all impossible prospects, and is ready to take him on a wild goose "show me" chase around town.

A number of years ago I was talking to an Idaho business man when a young fellow came dashing in and said, "Mr. Smith, I wish you'd let me take five dollars. I'll hand it to you in a day or two." Smith looked at him in silence for a minute or more, then turned, walked to the cash register, took out the five, gave it to him and said, "I wish you would just give this back to me—I have had it handed to me too much all ready." P. S. I hope this brings to your mind no unpleasant recollections.

The big business concerns of this country could save millions of dollars a year by making all Purchasing Agents sales managers. After they had read the reports of their salesmen for a while, showing that a good third of their salaries and expenses were wasted by having to await the pleasure of other purchasing agents to show their wares, they would likely have a little more respect for the time of salesmen calling upon them.

Having always minded my own business I have had only my own affairs that could worry me—and, they never have.

They tell me sea-faring men always know when to expect a school of sharks. So do I. When an automobile springs a leak and some fellow passing along, finds the damp spot and reports an oil discovery I know the best "schooled sharks" in the country are headed my way.

I never had a man object to my not smoking in his office, or around his place of business, so I just cultivated the habit of doing "open air" smoking, and I seem to get along all right.

There must be an end to all things, and this ends Just Plain Talk. If it has been helpful to you I am pleased. It is written "with malice toward none," and in the hope that it will be helpful. If it has done this, I am truly satisfied. Thank you.

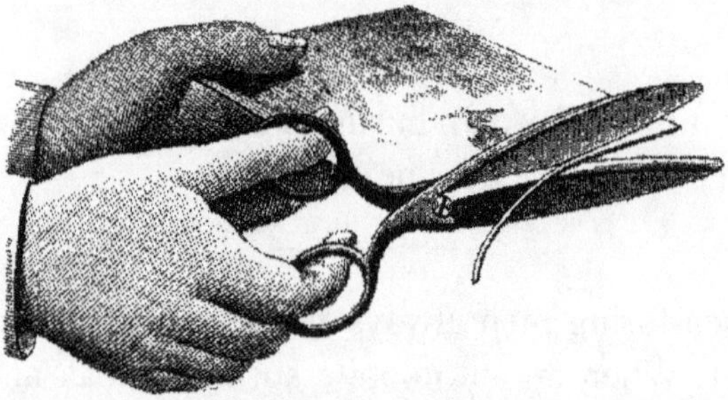

4

More Than Likely

There are many faults to be found in this little booklet—and, the right people are pretty sure to find them.

"Go To It"—or take what's coming.

You are going to be, that which you make out of what you are.

When we go grouching around, with the feeling that we deserve more than we get, we are pretty sure to get what we deserve.

Not until you quit excusing yourself, and accusing others of being responsible for your failures, will you ever amount to a hill of beans.

I would like mighty well to have some money, and when I think the price is right, I always try to lay in a few dollars, but darn my cat-skins if I'll pay the price, I see some fellows paying.

Look natural, and don't wait until you are in your coffin to do it.

Because they are fluent talkers, many young men get the idea they are natural born salesmen, when what nature intended them to be were barbers.

As he rushes through the main office he tells his operator to get you or me on the phone. She does, and then we wait, and wait, while she tries to locate him somewhere around the place. After many minutes, during which our business has been suspended, she tells us that Mr. No-Respect-for-Other-Men's-Time cannot be located, and that she will have to call again. Then I think what you think.

It takes the combined efficiency of a salesman, shipping clerk and accountant to make a customer.

Anyway, the fellow with his nose to the grindstone is not sticking it in somebody else's business.

An increase in overhead is usually brought about by an increase of swell-head.

It matters not what you are selling, you can never make it look any better to a prospective buyer than it looks to you.

I don't know, which is of the greatest value, Memory or Forgetfulness. While memory brings back my old friends, and the happy days of long ago, Forgetfulness puts out of mind the mistakes made, regrettable things said, and done, making life more enjoyable.

Overcoming adversity will bring you prosperity, and overcoming prosperity, will prove you to be a real man.

Can you call to mind a successful salesman who is not a conservative dresser, possesses a pleasing voice, and talks with sincerity that inspires confidence? Neither can I.

Your advertisement is an invitation extended business, to visit you. All depends on how you treat it, when it comes, as to how long it is going to stay.

In thinking back over your past life it is only the good deeds you have done, or those others have done you, that come to mind. Not the cold dollars you have made by some business transaction.

I have no use for "sob sisters," be they male, or female.

Clothes may not make a man, but did you ever see women giving smiles, and men passing cigars, to traffic cops when off duty, and dressed in citizen's clothes?

The first thing to learn about driving an automobile, is how to stop it. The same well applies to making an after dinner talk.

I have known more employees to refuse to leave the firm they were with to accept a position with a competitive firm at an increased pay, than I have known to accept such offers. Real human being treatment and little acts of kindness, along with expressions of appreciation, mean far more to a worthwhile employee, than a few more dollars.

Repeat orders usually come from salesmen having sold the clerks, who sell the consumers, that which the buyer bought.

Mercantile agencies can tell you what a man has, but his house servants can come nearer telling you what he is.

A merchant was telling me, that there was far more pleasure in pursuit than in possession. Remembering how he had run after me for my business until I gave it to him and the little attention he has since given it, I agreed with him.

Sprinkling the sidewalk with his tobacco juice, he said to me, "I'll tell you, we have a lot of laws that we need to enforce a blankety-blank sight more than this prohibition law." I said, "I think you are right, and I would suggest first the enforcement of the two you have just broken—spitting on the sidewalk, and using profanity in public."

We are governed by habits. Being honest and truthful are two of the best to cultivate.

About all a bass drummer does is mark time, and make a lot of noise. I have met a number of salesmen that missed their calling.

When a manufacturer produces the best piece of merchandise possible, and with advertising creates a demand for it, a man is confessing himself a mighty poor merchant, when he must offer the consumer his profit, in order to sell it.

When I receive a letter signed with a rubber stamp that reads, "Dictated but not read," or "Left the office before reading," I know it is from a "golf-hound."

Another good Declaration of Independence is a paid-up life insurance policy.

There are many times when an employer would like to give some employee an increase in salary, but does not do so, because he knows he would at once "confidentially" tell every other employee around the place, and have them all going around wearing grouches.

So many fellows that take advantage of opportunities, look upon their friends as being such.

Should your employer ever suggest you taking advantage of anyone in any manner whatever, quit him quick, and find another job. The selling of your personal respect and future, for a few dollars, is mighty poor business.

As sure as I become convinced that this old world is not using me any too well, and start feeling sorry for myself, here comes some blind man down the street, feeling his way with a stick, wearing a smile and whistling. Or some fellow with one, or both legs missing. Then, dogonit, I have to go back to being happy again.

Being a member of a church, fraternal and civic organization is no proof you are a real honest-to-goodness man. It only means you have been given an opportunity to associate with real men, that you may prove yourself to be one.

He stood upon the narrow sill, washing the window of my office from the outside, and on the tenth floor, without any safety device, whistling away, as though he was standing on the ground in perfect safety. I said to him, "Why don't you protect yourself with a strap?" In broken English he answered, "I have confidence in myself. When that is gone, I am gone." You don't have to be a window-washer to get the idea.

The man that hard work kills, is usually the fellow that accomplishes nothing.

When Tom Lee, the Memphis man who saved thirty people from drowning when a boat went down in the Mississippi river, was asked how he was able to accomplish such a seemingly impossible feat, he answered, "Well, Sir—Ah just kept on goin' after 'em 'n' git'n' 'em." I don't know but what salesmen would profit by adopting Tom's system.

When a salesman is paid less than he is worth, he is usually worthless.

When I see stenographers and switchboard operators on their way to work with library books and sewing baskets, I can better understand why Central gives the signal, "they don't answer."

I can remember when neighbors used to come in to spend the evening, and we would discuss books, music, art, civic and national affairs. But, civilization has advanced, and now we talk dieting, golf, new cars, the raising of other people's children, and wind it up with a game of bridge.

Right after delivering a ten-minute oration about the tipping evil, he told me what he thought of the firm he was with because they failed to give him a bonus check the first of the year.

Listing imaginary troubles of the day in the morning, and reading them over at the close of the day, after all have failed to happen, is a right good way to cure the worry habit.

The most talkative salesmen are those representing firms whose business methods cannot speak for themselves.

Real salesmanship is a cultivated gift of nature, and not a gift of gab.

Necessity is usually the messenger that brings a man his opportunity.
A leader is one who follows instructions.

The greatest waste of advertising money comes from the writing of that which will appeal to the vanity of the heads of the firm, in the place of being of enough interest to the prospective buyer to cause him to read it.

I expect there are banks in your town that you can't take a dime out of, because you never put a dime in them. And, more than likely there are a number of clubs and secret orders that you have joined, but are getting nothing out of, because you put nothing in them.

I hope that the talked-about contraption that will enable those talking over the phone to see the party at the other end will be perfected, for I would just like to have some of these stock salesmen see how I look when they call me up, and try to unload some "wild-cat" stuff on me.

Some sales managers surround themselves with "worshipers" in the place of workers.

Life's darkest moments for a man are those when he is standing in his own light.

Yes, the passing of the woodshed has had much to do with the increasing of business in juvenile court.

Lord preserve the "middle class" for it is they who give us our daily bread. Having our friendship, our friends give their business to our competitors, that they may make friends of them. Our enemies will not patronize us, so it is upon the "middle class" we must pin our faith.

Ever so often it is a good idea to take the square plugs out of the round holes by changing employees around to jobs they better fit.

Have you ever visited one of those so-called homes, where the furnishings were bought for show, and not for comfort, and felt as though you were in the display room of a furniture store, and were uncomfortable because you feared that occupying of one of the chairs might spoil its sale. So have I—and, I suppose that is why I feel so much at home at our house.

It occurs to me that, if space was more truthfully sold, the advertiser would not have to fill it with anything other than the truth in order to get his money back.

It is your standing with your firm earned by faithful service and loyalty, and not your "stand-in" with some manager of a department, that counts for something.

The poison-tongued "gas bags" we have in this country are killing off more good men and women every year than we need have any fear of being killed by foreign gas bags crossing the sea.

One drawer of my desk is given to personal letters from old friends, and when I want to free my mind of business, I take out one and answer it. The mental visit, and little chat I have with some friend in other parts is most refreshing and restful. And, I believe it causes me to put a little more friendly, human-being sort of feeling in the business letters I afterwards write.

Talk will keep an idle tongue going — but not a business.

When employees do not stay with a firm, customers seldom do.

I cannot think that all human beings are put together alike, the same as a dollar watch, and for that reason, I never get over excited when some fellow starts telling me, that I should live my life as he is living his. Some time ago, the world's greatest athlete stood before three hundred and more Rotarians in San Francisco, and told us how to live our lives, that we might become active, healthy men of old age. His own overtasked heart quit on him in less than ten days.

Have you an acquaintance whose every conversation starts or ends with, "sfunny thing." So have I. Met mine the other day and he said, "I saw a man and his wife killed in an automobile accident yesterday. Funniest thing I ever saw."

The masked footpad who meets you on a dark street, and tells you to "put 'em up" takes less of your time and money, than the one masked as a friend, who comes into your office and peddles you some worthless stock.

We will not see our faults, our friends never tell us of them, and our enemies glory in, and advertise them. So, taking it all in all, if we ever amount to much, it's almost an accident.

Cold coffee, charred toast, or the wind having blown the morning paper away, has caused me to hold off the making of many a sales talk until later in the day when the prospective buyer became normal.

A friend was telling me about some fellow having expressed a dislike for me. I answered, "Since we have only been acquainted a year, that means I lived fifty-three years without him. Having done that once, I ought to be able to do it again, and that would take me to the age of 106—possibly by that time I will not care."

A friend remarked, "See that man over there. He is worth a million dollars. To look at him you would not think it. He cares nothing for personal appearance, nor the pleasures of life, and he never gave a dollar to charity. And, yet he is worth a million dollars." I answered, "You mean he has a million dollars. He is not worth thirty cents."

When it takes some sort of a prize contest, a promised bonus, or the humiliating thoughts of not making a creditable showing along with other salesmen, to cause you to get out and sell—then you are a good man for your firm to get rid of.

After a glance, he passed it back to me, saying, "This may be advertising, but it don't appeal to me." I answered, "I am glad you noticed that. It was not written to appeal to you, but to those that are prospective buyers of that which you have to sell." He got the idea, and the advertising got the business.

I reckon I'm looked on as being hard-hearted, and more than likely I am, but try as I may, the sad tears will not come with a flow sufficient to wilt my collar, as some great big work-dodging young man, posing as an entertainer, parades around a cafe singing, "That dear old mother of mine."

Because of my many years experience in sales, I have often been asked, if I have any fixed rules for selling. I have, and here they are. First, I find out, who could with profit buy that which I have to sell. Then I find out for sure that they could pay for it in case they bought. Then I go ahead and make the sale.

What you don't know won't hurt you. But I get tired listening to it.

While the optimist is seeing the future, and the pessimist the past, is a good time for a real salesman to get out and see prospective buyers.

There is always a kind hearted old lady living in some hotel, who never knew what it was to be a housekeeper, that is ready to save the "down trodden working class" when the price of milk is advanced a cent a bottle, or bread a cent a loaf. The price per "rescue" is an interview and her picture on the front page of the newspaper.

Suppose you were to buy an automobile from a man, paying him his price for it. Then suppose that he would want to use it himself, just as he saw fit to do so. Then, suppose, again, you were to sell your time to a firm for so much per day, and—Well, you get the idea, don't you?

It is all wrong to assume that your friends know all about your business and will sooner or later give you an order. As example. Some years ago I was sent to a certain city to sell. I asked the local manager about a very large concern. He said, "The manager is a very close friend of mine, and when he is ready, he will come to me." I asked if I might call on him, and with a laugh, he gave his permission. The second call, I sold him one of the largest contracts ever written in the city.

You can better judge a man's religion by talking with his neighbors, than by his ability to memorize lodge rituals, and sing solos in church. When a man says "yes," he nearly always knows what HE is talking about, but when he says "no" he doesn't know what YOU are talking about.

Not until you put selfishness out of your life, can you hope to bring happiness into it.

When I am asked right quick as to what it takes to make a salesman, I answer "brains and feet."

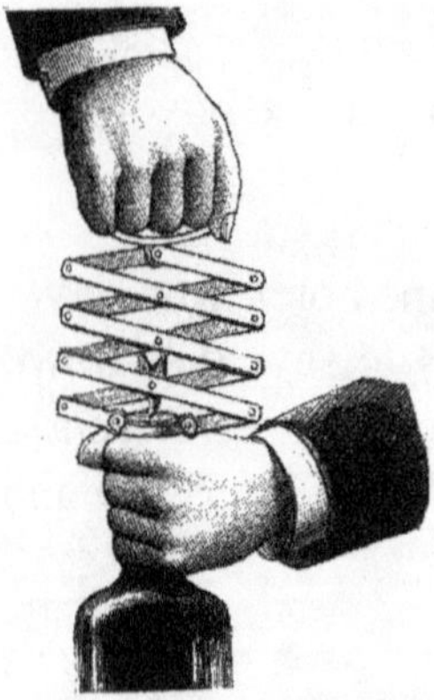

To reach Success you've got to go straight. Every crooked turn you make lengthens the trip.

Not that I am at all in sympathy with young "speeders," at the same time, before Dad "kicks up too much fuss" about Billy's having stepped on the gas, it might be well for him to call to mind the way he used to lay the whip to Old Dobbin, sending him through the streets at a "break-neck speed," which in those days was just about as dangerous.

William Brown wanted to perpetuate the name he had carried through life, so when the first offspring arrived, he was given the name of William Brown, Jr. As a result, he finds himself at middle age known by all as "Old Bill Brown" while the youngster is "Young Bill."

I don't know but there is more to be gained by studying those who have failed than in trying to follow in the footsteps of the successful.

Another thing that ought to be done, is to have a municipal siren blow every afternoon at four-thirty, to let all "do nothing gad-abouts" know they have thirty minutes' time in which to take a street car for home, before the seats are needed for tired workers.

Yes, travel is a real education. One day aboard a Pullman, with occasional visits to the smoking compartment, or club car, will teach a fellow more vulgarity and profanity, than he would learn in months around home.

Nearly every employer remembers what Sis Hopkins said about "there ain't nothing in doin' nothin' for nobody that ain't doin' nothin' for you." That is why a lot of employee's salaries are never increased. P. S. And it is often the reason employees do not do more work.

I hope I will never accumulate enough money to cause me to feel I can disregard my personal appearance, and go around looking like a tramp.

Yessiree, "Opportunity knocks at every man's door" and it keeps on knocking for those that keep on hearing.

"When I make up my mind, that settles it" is a common expression among those that have settled at the bottom of the ladder.

"No man ever gets too old to learn" and few ever become old enough to do so.

Any time you mail a business man a poorly mimeographed letter, in a cheap envelope, bearing second-class postage, with the thought he will place no further value on it than you do, and pass it to the waste basket unread—you win.

Keep asking questions. You will never meet a man who cannot tell you something worth while that you do not know, however humble his position in life may be.

It is said, "Every man is entitled to his own opinion," and so he is. All would be well, if he would keep it, and not insist upon imposing it upon others.

If you need it—really want it—have the money—and can spare it—why, doggone it—go and buy it. It is not what you deny yourself, but that which you can buy yourself, that will add to your life's comforts.

One time I saw a sign in an office that read, "Keep everlastingly at it." From the way things looked, I would say it was put up on a holiday.

Yesterday is of no further value to you today than to use in estimating your worth tomorrow.

The best way to hold your job is to Work. Few are looking for that sort of a job.

Because excitement expelled fear from the mind, many a man wears a hero medal.

As long as we employ six thousand dollar a year attorneys to enforce our laws, and others at fifty and a hundred thousand a year to defeat them, it's a fine chance justice has.

The sort of reformers we need in this country are those who live lives so clean and happy that others will want to imitate them.

It is said, that talking to yourself is an indication of insanity. Where a fellow is excusing himself of his faults, or congratulating himself upon his greatness, I feel there is some truth in it.

Save all your surplus sympathy, for the man who works for an unreasonable boss, and is married to another one.

In stores where customers buy and are not sold there is little need for a refund and exchange department.

More than likely your ideas as to how the business should be run are right, and those of your employer wrong, but if I were you, I would go right on doing what he wants done; then when he fails, he can't blame you. P. S.—Besides that, you'll have better luck holding your job.

I once said to a man, "For six months you have been doing your darndest to think up excuses for not doing business with me, and now I want you to use ten minutes of the same sort of hard thinking of some one reason for doing business with me." He smiled—said he would—did—and, bought.

John Ray lived in the little Kentucky town I was raised up in. For years and years, John fished Salt River, a little stream where the fish were few and small. Everyone caught fish except John. He would use the very largest hooks he could buy, contending he was going to have big fish, or no fish at all. The last time I was back to the old home town, I learned John was dead, and I asked, "Did he ever land a big fish?" I was told he did not. So often when I see young men loafing the streets, supported by their relatives, or living off of money borrowed from friends, waiting to land some big job, in the place of taking what they can get, I think of John Ray having never caught a fish.

If you want to find out what is wrong with the world, do not ask those that are wrong.

Every man looks upon it as a pleasure to befriend someone, and would gladly take advantage of every chance to do so, if he thought he could have as an epitaph for his headstone the slogan used by many second-hand car dealers — "Used but not Abused."

Good or bad—get it out of you.

I have read several books by memory experts telling how to call men by their right names. Strikes me, that more men would be called by their right names if they would pay their debts, keep their promises, and attend strictly to their own business.

It's time enough to say it, when you know it to be true.

Applying energy in holding the job you have will conserve a greater energy in seeking another one.

A friend insisted I do business with a certain bank because they were the most liberal in the city in making loans. I told him I had often heard that said, and that was my one best reason for not banking with them.

The more you put off doing things that ought to be done, the more likely your employer is to put on someone else to do them.

The average fellow asking for advice, really wants someone to tell him what he wants to hear.

Anyone can be happy by thinking of all they have that should bring happiness.

The popularity of the automobile has not lessened the value of "horse sense" in the least.

Boats, trains and aeroplanes will get you where you want to go, but truth, honesty and dependability will get you where you want to be.

When an automobilist begins to slow down and take it easy, that is the time for you to go ahead of him. P.S. Read that over again, substituting the word "employee" for automobilist."

Many a favorable impression created by attractive windows, clean store and well arranged stock, has been all shot to pieces when the groceries were delivered from a dirty unsanitary-looking wagon, by a driver whose personal appearance matched the wagon.

A chronic grumbler once said to me, "If you'll listen, you'll agree I have a 'kick' coming." I listened, and felt like giving it to him.

I can't see where the inventor of the new "lie detector" machine expects to find a market for the thing for I know of no married man but what has one.

To mend your ways, commence by making good all broken promises. When your employer finds out he can bank on you —you will bank more.

The so-called "white lies" that fall from your lips, like the white snowflakes falling upon a factory roof in Pittsburgh, do not stay white very long.

When the unaccused start making a defense, it's time to be looking for guilt.

When an optimistic manufacturer unloads his over-production on the wholesaler, he overstocks the retailer, who to rid himself of it, sells it to the consumer on credit. The consumer cannot pay the retailer, the retailer the wholesaler, the wholesaler the manufacturer, the manufacturer his banker—And, there you are.

The difference between you and other men is nothing more than that part of you that you make.

Among my greatest worries are these fellows who deliver a lecture at every opportunity on why I should not worry.

The salesman with the longest legs may make the greatest number of calls, the one with the longest tongue the most talks, but the one with the longest head will keep on making the greatest number of sales.

I have frequently noticed metal plates on door steps that read, "No Peddlers," and I always felt that I could increase the happiness of the home by adding—"of Gossip Need Enter."

A college education does one of two things for a young man. It makes him a bigger and better man--or a more complete ass.

"Credit to those whom credit is due" was but an old expression until R.G. Dun printed their names in book form, and now its popularity among credit men who want to know who they are, keeps it among the seven best sellers.

Owing to owing, many lose jobs.

When a salesman gets in order mentally and morally orders will come along regularly.

I can always tell when a letter has been one-fingered by the writer. He pens after his signature, "Please excuse this very poorly written letter. Am trying out a new girl."

Know your work, and do it Well, ever remembering that where ignorance is bliss—men lose jobs.

With some, the making of money is looked upon as a gift, and friends and relatives borrowing it, look upon it in the same way.

I never ask a traveling salesman about general business conditions in a city. I ask him if he sold any goods there, and that gives me the answer to the first question in far less time.

If your business judgment had been fifty-one per cent right in the past, you would be golfing your winters away in Florida, giving small boys pennies to be used as foundations upon which to build fortunes.

Success is achievement. The reward incidental.

The best proof I have to offer that I am entitled to your friendship, is the sort of people who are my enemies.

Salesmen that keep on looking for business are as sure to find it as are those that are looking for insults.

I once heard a lady say, "My husband never once gave me candy or flowers before we were married, but I have never known what it was to be without either since then." Thank goodness it was my wife that said it.

Along during the day, repeat to yourself, that which the street car conductor was calling out on your way to work—"There's plenty of room up in front."

My friends have given me the happiness I have enjoyed and I credit them with whatever business success I have had, but I alone am responsible for my failures.

We don't know what we would have done, or what we would do, were we living the lives of others, so what is the use of talking about the mistakes they made, when we can make so much better use of the time in correcting our own?

When a speaker or a writer, in order to create laughter, attempts to ridicule another man's religion or nationality—he is about through.

Regrets generally come so late in life they are of little use. There is but one way to avoid old man Regret and that is to do just as near right as you know how all the time.

I reckon the reason some people don't like sparrows, is because there are so darn many of 'em. Maybe that's the reason they don't like poor folks.

We are all more or less self-appointed traffic cops on the road of life, trying to tell others which road to take.

How is a poor youngster going to say his prayers at mother's knee, if she has them under a card table or against the back of a seat at a picture show?

A successful man is one who has accomplished that which he started out in life to do, and is doing it better than most anyone else has ever done it. He may be your banker, then again, he might be your barber.

It is going to be mighty hard to make some fellows believe that a dog is man's best friend, for what does a dog know about endorsing notes and slipping a fellow a ten spot?

Wake up, and give your dreams a chance to come true.

I suppose it is just as well the newspapers only print the names of those "held up" by footpads, and not those that are being held up by friends and relatives.

Envy and jealously are at the bottom of all unkind things said. When we are hearing nothing but flattery about ourselves, we can take it to mean we are that which no one cares to be, and have nothing they want.

When you are on the level, you are above the average.

The only way to have others forget your mistakes of the past, is to so live the present, their thoughts will be your future success.

For a long time I have been preaching the doctrine "That we get out of life just what we put into it." A neighbor of mine heard me make this statement several times, and one day took me to task as follows: "Say Cox, tell me how you are ever going to collect from these little sparrows and robins and wild canaries I see you feeding every morning?" "Well," I replied, "I don't know how or where or when, but you can rest assured I will be paid in full all right." He just laughed and went on, but a few mornings later he stopped and was admiring the roses in our garden, when all of a sudden he discovered there were no bugs on our bushes and right away he wanted to know what kind of spray we used, declaring the bugs were destroying every plant he had. I told him we had never used a spray, and explained it to him after this fashion. "You see we have a hundred or more birds breakfast with us every morning and they sing us a song or two, but they do not seem to feel that their songs are pay enough for what we do for them, and in wanting to do more, they have undertaken the job of freeing our plants of insects, that they may not destroy them as they have yours. It always works that way. We get out of life just what we put into it." With a smile he said, "Cox, you win."

When a man tells you he is busy as a bee, it's well to remember a bee is his busiest when trying to sting somebody.

Be very careful in selecting the firm you are to work for. Your social standing, and your credit is rated by the firm you are associated with. So, select one that has a reputation above reproach, and so live your life as to add credit to its reputation, thereby showing your appreciation of the opportunity given you to share it.

If you are my friend, why should I ask you to grieve and worry with me because of my ailments and troubles, when your doing so could not relieve me of either? If you are not my friend, then why give you the satisfaction of knowing I am in trouble? Eliminating our friends and enemies, we have none left to whom we may tell our troubles, and that is a mighty fine fix to be in.

Go right on with your dream of "self importance," but my advice is, you stop, look, and listen at railroad crossings in the place of sounding your horn.

Exaggeration is misrepresentation, and misrepresentation is nothing more than downright lying, and lying never made a success of man or business.

Doing something for someone will bring you more happiness than doing someone for something.

Many run bills awhile—then bills run them.

You have met men with pockets so loaded with trash they could not find anything they wanted when they wanted it. The same fellows usually have their minds so filled with non-essentials there is no parking space for a worthwhile thought.

Nature opens the eyes of a kitten nine days after birth; many men grow old in years, then have some adventuress open theirs.

When a boy, you were given a bigger suit, when you outgrew the one you had. The same thing is going to apply to the position you are given in the business world.

It is always the employees that you hear singing around a place of business.

One young man wished to be successful—one worked to be—one was.

The easiest way to sweeten your disposition is to free your mind of bitter thoughts.

I had rather look upon all men as being honest, and lose a bet now and then, than live a life of suspicion and distrust.

It is said, "imitation is the sincerest flattery." Maybe so. But, when a man creates something, that the public considers worthwhile, and is about to reap some little reward for his efforts, it is right hard for him to appreciate the "flattery" of impostors.

I never had a man object to my not smoking in his office, or around his place of business, so I just cultivated the habit of doing "open air" smoking, and I seem to get along all right.

Before a man erects a skyscraper, or presents his city with a library, park or something of the sort to perpetuate his memory, he should remember that people have a habit of asking, "How did he get his money?"

When employing men or women for sales or office work it is well to remember that conservative dressers are conservative thinkers.

Sensible men are seldom sensitive.

We usually hear enough of the truthful things said about us to others, to overcome the flattering things said to us.

Everything of real worth is bought with self-sacrifice.

A Washington, D.C., speaker, in addressing a San Francisco audience said, "Coleman Cox has the advantage of most writers. He is an advertising man, and the advertising he writes for his books well describes their contents. I had a friend that wrote a book. Months passed, and he had not sold enough copies to pay his proof-reader. I advised him to find a good advertising writer, have him write a number of ads, and run them in some of the leading magazines. He did, and got immediate results. One man wrote, 'I read your ad, bought your book, and have just finished reading it. I have but one fault to find. Why in the dickens didn't you have the man that wrote the ad write the book?'"

It is easy enough to believe that "tomorrow never comes" until your banker advises that your note, due tomorrow, cannot be renewed; or the tax collector notifies you that tomorrow is the last day you have to pay your taxes—then you had better make some arrangements for its coming.

5

Think It Over

Editor's note:
This chapter originally appeared as a booklet entitled *Think It Over*. The following is Coleman Cox's original introduction to that booklet:

> *What is Success? Surely the most successful business man in the world can best answer that question, and in "Think it Over" Mr. Henry Ford does answer it, in the first personally written article of the kind ever printed over his signature.*
>
> *There is another message in "Think it Over" by Mr. Irving T. Bush, President of the Chamber of Commerce of the State of New York, head of the Bush Terminal Company, and noted writer on economics, that should be memorized by every young man and woman of the business world.*
>
> *Along with these two wonderful articles I offer two hundred or more paragraphs, telling something of my experiences and observations in business life, which I hope you will enjoy.*
>
> \- Coleman Cox

HENRY FORD

Detroit, Michigan

What is success? It is fulfilling your own measure and maybe enlarging it a little. Every man when he is born is a prophecy of some satisfying career; success is the fulfillment of that prophecy. It may be in one way, it may be in another; it may be involved, in the accumulation of material wealth, it may be in the performance of services more fruitful to others than to oneself—in any case, success is fulfilling oneself.

But people will not believe that at once. One needs to be successful in the conventional way to learn just how far away from success it may be. I do not believe that material accumulation is the whole of success, and on the other hand I do not believe that true success ever excludes a sufficient possession of wealth. But wealth as a means, not as an end. Some men are called successful because they have accumulated enough money to enable them to live without working. And, strange to say, many people are looking forward to the day when they will have enough to live without working. Wealth is the end they seek; wealth to them is not a means of doing still greater things with, it is the success itself.

Well, when a man reaches this point he is a failure. He is a mental and a moral failure. Any man who can live without work —live in any sense at all—is a down-and-outer, however rich he may be. Anyone whose interest in life and the work of life is so weak that he lives in hopes of some day being able to live without work is already headed for failure, no matter how successful he may be in hoarding money. Money that represents hoarding is not wealth anyway; money that represents service is the means to greater service.

There are no rules for success. Every man's own personal pattern of success is born with him, and the rules too. He must think; it is the hardest possible work, and most people refuse to do it—but he must think, and the rules of his life will become plain. And then he must follow his destiny. The only good that "stories of success" can do is to confirm your faith that success is the natural destiny of all of us; they cannot give you the rules. One man's rule is another man's ruin. And, likewise, every story of failure teaches us how utterly needless it was.

The fundamental faith of life is this—you were put here for a purpose, to do something; and doing it will be your success.

Charge up every experience as profit, and push on. When you find your place, don't settle in it—widen it, push it on. Success is constant ongoing, ceaseless growth. Life is motion. Forward motion is unavoidable in success.

- Henry Ford

IRVING T. BUSH
President of Chamber of Commerce of the State of New York
Head of Bush Terminal Co. and Noted Writer on Economics

I wish I could show young men and women some easy road to success—but there is none. You may think you see someone traveling it, but if it is easy it is not permanent. It is only one of those rises which make the fall all the harder. Success cannot be without character and character grows as your muscles grow through exercise. Honesty and dependability are absolutely essential to any permanent success.

The chief cause of failure is the fact that few young men set out for a definite goal. Life seems sort of a joy ride and they are tempted into every byroad that looks attractive. In the beginning, a young man who starts with little must learn to live within that little, and save something. He can never be happy and comfortable if he lives beyond his means and does not use sane judgment in providing for the unknown future.

Religion and self-discipline are important. I do not mean religion in the technical observance of the precise methods of worship laid down by any specific church. I mean religion in a belief in an over-ruling power for good, and in the rightness of being honest and kind and clean. Unless a man has that kind of religion in him he will not be a success, even though he accumulates a vast fortune. You have asked me to name ten successful men. I will not do so, because their names would mean nothing to you or your readers. They would not be the names of men who had achieved great positions in the world. They would be the names of men who are filling their jobs as well as they possibly can be filled, are maintaining a happy home, and getting and giving their share of real happiness in life.

- Irving T. Bush

When Opportunity knocks, there is little need of you going to the door unless you have prepared for its coming by saving up a few dollars.

The poor-house is populated with people who tried to live their lives according to the incomes of others.

You are a successful athlete when you can "carry" a bank account, "lift" drafts or mortgages, and "vault" life insurance policies and other good securities.

"How can I get ahead?" is the question that is bothering those who have heads they are not using.

A young promoter was telling me how foolish I was to be putting money in a savings bank where I would get but four per cent, when by buying his stock I would get at least ten or twelve. I told him I didn't figure I was losing anything, as I was charging the difference up to the restful sleep I was enjoying.

You don't have to know how to sing, it's the feeling as though you want to, that makes the day a successful one.

The best way to get the attention of a prospective buyer is to give him yours for it.

Letters of recommendation are often much the same as epitaphs on tombstones. Kind words said to cheer along the "dead ones" that are to be with us no more.

Luther Burbank had worked for three years in perfecting a plant, the bloom was on it, and soon seed were to be taken, and another of his wonderful creations would be given the world, when a woman he had granted permission to visit his gardens plucked it. I know another like case. A salesman had worked for years in securing a very desirable account for his firm, and just as things were getting started off nicely, a "swivel chair executive" in the sales department who never made a sale in his life wrote him an uncalled for letter.

If you do anything worth talking about—let somebody else do the talking.

As an expression of friendliness a man smiles and a dog wags his tail. I have never had a dog with a wagging tail bite me, but I have been "bit" a number of times by smiling salesmen.

I don't care to hear anything about my mistakes of yesterday, but if you have any inside information on any I might make tomorrow—pass it along.

Promptly adjust all complaints, and if a customer wants his money back, give it to him with a smile—if it cracks your face to do it. It's your only way of getting the money back in your cash register.

Advertising pays—when both the buyer and seller profit.

The Rotarians started preaching it, then other like clubs, composed of business men, took it up, and now everybody is asking everybody as to what this so called "service" really means. I'll tell just exactly what it means—it means that the time has come for you to make use of the Golden Rule in your business.

It is said "It takes three generations to make a gentleman." Yes, and then he rushes into a street car—parks himself in the only vacant seat—buries his face in a paper—while some old lady—an elderly gentleman—or a mother with a baby in her arms, swings on a strap over him. Then the work of three generations is all shot to pieces.

I want to always want, and I'll never be satisfied to be satisfied.

As the poor old ragged bum bowed his thanks and moved on my friend said to me:—"I always give old Tom a piece of silver. I knew him as a boy, as a prosperous young man, and I often call to mind his expression: `Have a good time while you're young, and when you get old—keep it up." When I see a young man whose only thought is a "good time" I picture "a hard time" ahead for a certain old man.

When a fellow thinks he is "putting it over" on the boss, the boss is not thinking of putting him over others as boss.

Well, there is this consolation: When you have no money there are no "high-pressure" salesmen around pestering you about buying "wild-cat" oil or mining stock. No income tax reports to bother with—your wife has no thought of divorcing you to get half of what you haven't—and no girl is going to sue you for breaking her heart a few hundred thousand dollars worth.

Did you ever have one of these fellows, who hurry in to make a loan, ever hurry to return it? Neither did I.

To those young men entering business life expecting immediate success, it might be well to say, that fully one-third of the members of the New York Rotary Club held obscure positions until they passed forty: after which they achieved high executive positions.

It is so much easier to hold the job you have than it is going to be to find another one. I have noticed, that when a fellow is entitled to a better job, it comes to him, and he doesn't have to go around looking for it.

The best book of advice I know anything about tells us exactly in whom we can place our trust, but we've gone ahead trusting to luck, relatives, stock salesmen, and supposed friends—and—well, you know what's happened.

"Let's go" is the right sort of a spirit for a young fellow just starting business life to have, but as soon as he finds the job he fits he should forget it, because many the young man "lets go" just about the time he should be holding on.

No, I don't think I am confessing myself old or old fashioned when I say that I nearly always feel the need of a mental and a moral bath after seeing the average moving picture show.

A politician needs followers while a business man must have leaders in order to succeed.

When a fellow stops trying—he starts lying.

Sales contests often bring in orders from firms never before sold—and, before the money is collected the firm wishes they never had been.

Most people seem to think "Am I my brother's keeper" is a personal question jailers and keepers of insane asylums alone should answer.
It is the business of lawyers, doctors and bankers to listen to, and relieve you of your troubles, and if they can't do anything for you—why tell 'em to me.

The salesman who thinks he can't, usually gets the "Can't" without the "t."

A young man's life troubles have commenced when he starts borrowing money to buy the non-essentials of life.

Three men were seated on a bench in a park—Two of them were telling what was wrong with the business world—The other one was broke and out of a job, too.

You can't hope for success—You've got to "hop" for it.

Mr. Rodin didn't help the world along much when he made his "Thinker" in a sitting posture. The fellow that does his thinking these days sitting around with elbow resting on knee and chin on fist is going to get run over by those who are on their way to "do something" and are thinking out a way to do it while on the way.

You run no risk of getting into any argument, when you tell a man that his success can well be attributed to his good business judgment, and hard work, while the greater success of his friends is nothing more than luck.

An easy way to find out whether a fellow is on his way "up," or "out," is to ask him what sort of a man his employer is.

When a fellow, who has, for years, had the exclusive sale of some well known product, loses his job and has to take out a line that has strong competition—Oh Boy!

I think it was a great mistake to give some men both tongues and brains, for having one they seldom use the other.

If you have a business that can't get along without you for a few days, then the undertaker ought to collect from you in advance.

I don't know but what the Frenchman has the right idea. That is to say, I had just about as soon have a fellow kiss me on each cheek as to fill one of my ears with his imaginary troubles, the other with his ailments.

When told you need to exercise, it is just possible your adviser means mental and not physical exercise, or feels you could exercise a little more judgment in overcoming evil with good.

The firm you are working for receives any number of magazines and trade papers containing wonderful articles written by the best posted and most successful men in your line of business. That is nothing new to you. Nor is it news that you have never asked the loan of any of them over night, that you might read them and become a better man, worthy of promotion and more money than you are getting.

When you think you are in trouble, the trouble is in you.

In reconstructing the dictionary I would suggest that the word Alimony be listed as a reason for getting married—and divorced.

It is not the going to college, but what you come away with that counts.

"The devil gets his dues," and so does the young man who gets the idea in his head he's a "regular devil."

Many a man credited with writing good business letters should have Lloyds write him a policy on his reputation, for it would be a total loss were his Secretary to quit him.

Vaudeville performers, knowing they are going to have to come back, hold their best for the encore. Not so with the average salesman. He tries to tell everything he knows the first interview.

"Love thy neighbor as thyself" is looked upon by some as being impossible because they think it refers to the fellow living next door who raises chickens that do their scratching in their gardens—starts pushing a lawn mower at six-thirty Sunday morning, and has a half dozen bad youngsters he makes no effort to control.

Unless you do a little thinking and planning tonight you are not going to be any better man tomorrow than you were today.

Fear is an Oregon Boot on the leg of progress.

The man who minds his own business and leaves it entirely up to other people to look after their own affairs really has very little to worry about.

Some men lie with words—others with pleasant smiles—and friendly hand-shakes.

When an employee loses his temper he never advertises for it. He advertises for another job.

There are some things no man can do, and they are the things he THINKS he can't do.

Suppose a retail salesman were to approach a customer and make the same sales talk the advertising man has written and printed, and suppose the advertising man were to print the salesman's talk—I say—suppose.

We credit successful men with being quick thinkers. Not always so. What they do is to act on first thought, while others want to think it over. Our first thoughts are usually our best, and when we do not use them, doubt, the mother of fear, steps in, and fear always has, and always will, stand between us and success.

The best investment a young man can make is to buy a five or ten thousand dollar bank account on the installment plan. A small payment down, and a few dollars each month will pay for it in a few years. Think it over.

I suppose, you too, meet many fellows who can remember when they could have bought an acre of land right in the heart of the city for less money than a few feet now sell for. But, before you waste any tears over their "losses" remember they had no more money with which to buy the acre, than they now have to buy a few feet.

When you are listed among "Who's Who" you will be in a position to say "What's What."

Time spent in looking for faults in others could best be used in correcting our own.

We all want the newspapers to print the truth—so long as they leave our names out of it.

A business doesn't happen—it's a thing we make.

When I see a fellow showing up late for work, and sneaking away early, I am reminded of the two men who were reading the epitaphs on tombstones through the iron fence of a cemetery. One read from a large monument, "John W. Brown, not dead but sleeping." The other man said, "Not dead but sleeping—Eh. Say, that man ain't kidding nobody 'cept himself."

I have known many a good man to be no good.

Too many young men want credit for more than they do, and accept credit for more than they can pay.

A cigarette manufacturer got right mad about something I said in one of my books regarding cigarette smoking, but inasmuch as he makes and sells them, and I do the smoking and morning coughing, I still contend I knew what I was talking about.

An education is something like the flu—all those having chances, don't get it.

The law says the pedestrian is entitled to the right of way, but having the law on your side, and a ton truck on your back is a darn bad combination.

There are merchants who are always glad to see certain salesmen come in, because they want to hear the latest story. Then there are other salesmen they are glad to see come in because they want to give them some orders.

The "Back to the Farm" movement has gone over big. Too big for the good of the country. It looks as though every farmer's son is turning his "back to the farm" and facing for some city.

You have heard one person in church, or at a theatre cough, and start all others to coughing, and, you have seen a person yawn and start others to doing so. Then again you have seen smiles that put others to smiling, and you have met happy people who made you happy—Do you get the idea?

For a year or more we lived in the same hotel. He knew who I was—I knew who he was—He'd look at me—I at him—Then one day somebody said "Mr. Jones this is Mr. Cox"—and ever since then we have been good friends. I have often thought of my going without his friendship for a year just because of "damphool formality."

Quit making excuses and start making good.

Many a father sends a perfectly good son to college and only gets a "half" or a "quarterback."

Work eight hours, play eight hours and sleep eight hours; but if you want to hold your job, don't try to do all three between the hours of 9 A. M. and 5 P. M.

The only things that "come to you" that are worth anything are thoughts to be used in "going after" the things you want.

The "situation reports" some salesmen send in fool their Sales Managers about as much as toupees fool you and me.

Mr. Irving T. Bush was telling me about a friend of his who employed five hundred men, and because of business conditions found it necessary to drop a hundred from the payroll. Not wanting to discharge any of those who were interested in their work, he secured the names of those first to appear in the washroom to make ready to dash out of the building immediately the hour hand pointed to five, and as their names appeared they were discharged.

The only time some men ever have an opinion is when they are called for jury duty.

When the prospective buyer is not a willing and interested listener, you are wasting a sales talk.

When I hear the "never had a chance" yelp of a failure I can but think Edison never had a phonograph or an electric light—Ford didn't have an automobile, and Wright Bros. had no aeroplane until they made one. You can take it from me, boy, you'll never have a chance until you make it.

I think sales managers are all wrong in making new salesmen believe that the selling of their merchandise is but an order taking proposition for a half dozen "turn downs" kills their enthusiasm and they are ready to quit.

Talk about your scare-head advertising—out here in San Francisco a minister had a large sign painted and put up over the door of his Church, that read :—"Don't wait for a hearse to bring you to Church." Bygeorge, I'll say this for him—he put me to thinking.

Many a fellow considers himself a salesman because through sympathy his personal friends give him enough business to hold him his job.

We are entirely too liberal. We give too much time to worrying about the affairs of others, and in giving others advice we should be taking.

You will have less worries, when you have no secrets of your own, and refuse to be trusted with those of others.

Sometimes I wonder if all the politeness in the average place of business should be behind the counter. Wouldn't it help if the buyer were considerate, and as affable as he thinks the salesman should be.

Do you remember when you were a boy how easy it was to coast down a hill, and what an effort it was to get back to the top again. It is well you remember, because the experience ought to be worth something to you in your business life.

When I was a boy I had one of the best rabbit running dogs in Kentucky. The funny thing about it was, he didn't want the rabbit when he'd catch it but was ready to run another one. Well, sir, I so often think of that fool dog when I see men who have accumulated one fortune, another, and another, and are running themselves to death to get another one.

You will never amount to much so long as you worry about the amount you are paid.

About the only things that are given us these days are cold cures, political and religious opinions.

Another thing I have never been able to get through my head is, how can a man figure himself a salesman when he can't sell his own services, and wants you and me to unload him on some of our business friends.

The secret of success in selling is a man's ability and honest desire to put himself in the buyer's place.

When you are looking for sympathy you are not liable to find business.

Of course there is this way of looking at it too—If you are not young and good looking enough to cause a man to give you his seat on a street car—you have the satisfaction of knowing he does not look upon you as being old enough to need it.

I have been a salesman, and sales manager for more than thirty years. I have seen all sorts of contests, bonus schemes, etc., tried out, but my experience has been that the most loyal workers, and dependable producers are those who are paid what their services are worth in real money on the first of the month without ifs and ands.

Another thing that would help me forget about those pre Volstead days would be for telephone operators to take the limberness out of their tongues in saying "T-H-R-E-E."

The click, click, click of the wheels on the rails tell you that you are getting nearer and nearer the end of your journey—and—the tick, tick, tick of the clock tells you the same sort of a story.

When one of those fellows, wearing the same smile of sincerity as that used by a floor walker, and possessing the modesty of a politician, applies for a job as salesman—stay off of him.

Going to church on Sunday is not going to be worth much to you unless it regulates "your going" the following six days of the week.

Some salesmen know nothing whatever about scientific salesmanship, and if it wasn't for their bringing in more orders than those that do, the chances are they'd all be out of jobs.

Money may not mean success, but it is often necessary to have something that represents it when you approach a banker for a loan.

The employee who is constantly complaining about not getting what is coming to him usually gets it.

It is not so hard to believe that a good wife is often responsible in one way or another for the success of a man when we try to call to mind the bachelors whose names stand out as having accomplished something worth while in life.

They were talking about a certain lawyer, and some one remarked that he was a very smart man. My father-in-law said "Yes he's smart, but its damn mean smartness." Likely you, too, know of a few of the same kind.

The salesman who knows what he's talking about has but little to say.

Men become successful by being careful and remain successful only so long as they are careful.

To some fellows, Faith, Hope and Charity means:—having Faith in the Hope that they will not be asked to give to Charity.

Keep trying, it is often the last key you try that opens the door.

When some people come to you for advice, or information, they seem to feel, that in order to show you they are interested in what you are trying to tell them, they must interrupt you every half minute and politely call you a liar, by saying—"Zatso?" —"You don't tell me," "You can't mean it" and "I can't believe you." Then you feel like saying "Oh! Wotsthause."

I think there is something in this Coue doctrine, I believe that the man who can honestly say to himself at the close of the day's work :—"Day by day in every way I am getting better and better" will get where he started for a few jumps ahead of the other fellow.

Yes, I too have heard a lot of business men say that when they pulled down the top of the desk they forgot all about business until the next day. Like you I never believed them.

The best way to get the job of the fellow ahead of you is by helping him get a better one.

Remember that only you and your closest personal friends know about your wealth, and when you go around dressed like a "bum" all those that do not know you intimately look upon you as being one.

It was five o'clock—the employees whose day's work was done were passing through the Main Office—on their way home—with that happy "nothing to do until tomorrow" feeling. As they glanced in the Director's Room, they saw the Officers who were assembling for an important conference that would likely last far into the night. As the employees looked at their employers each thought, "When I get where they are, I will be happy." As the executives looked at the employees they thought, "When I was where they are, I was happy."

I have no sympathetic tears to shed for the fellow who invests his money in some sort of a "sure-thing game" by which he expects to get something for nothing—and gets nothing.

The success of Grand Opera singers, and vaudeville performers, depends greatly upon their being properly dressed to play their parts. This truth might be worth something to dentists, lawyers, doctors, salesmen, office workers, and all others in professional, and business life.

Many employees look upon a promotion as being a soft job, big pay and lots of authority. The "exercising" of authority usually ends the dream in a short while.

I have never known but one cure for nervousness and fear, with which so many salesmen are affected—Truth and Honesty.

Before you ask for an increase in salary be sure you have it coming to you and can conclusively prove it to your employer. Then if you don't get it—quit—for you'll never be worth two whoops to the firm or yourself by staying on the job.

I list as the meanest and most selfish man I ever knew the manager of a business who objected to a poorly paid girl in his office having a ten dollar a month increase, that he might, by keeping down operating expenses, secure a better salary for himself.

So many sales conferences remind me of service stations, where more gas is taken on for another trip.

It takes that which you "go after" to offset that which you have coming to you.

At least nine out of every ten, so called, secrets are cowardly lies.

Somebody was telling me of a young fellow who conceived the idea the firm he was with could not well get along without him, and made known, to his employer, the fact that he was going to quit, unless he was given an immediate and substantial increase in salary. His boss answered him by singing the second line of "Hail; Hail, the Gang's All Here."

Editor's note: That second line is "What the deuce do we care?"

To be happy, appreciate more the things you have and worry less about the things you have not.

Have you ever tried looking upon Life as a firm with which you have an account whereby you are charged with the wrongs you do and are credited with the good deeds done? And before closing your eyes on a finished day, do you ever look over its pages to see if you have any credits with which to start another day? I find this a pretty good idea. Suppose you try it.

If you will take the bull by the horns you will get along better than you will by trying to peddle it.

I have met quite a few employees who frankly confessed they knew more about the running of the business than their employers and, I have met a lot of old maids and bachelors who were authority on the raising of children. P. S. I think the same thing that you think about them.

A conscience, like the taste for olives, needs to be cultivated.

All any firm asks, or expects of a new employee is that he be 50% of what he claims to be when he applied for the job.

Some years ago I called on a manufacturer to interest him in advertising. He had a reputation among salesmen as being the meanest man in town to approach. No sooner had I announced my business, when he said "I throw a dozen advertising men out of this office every day." I answered, "Well, if this system of yours becomes general, and others begin throwing your salesmen out, how long do you expect to stay in business?" Evidently he hadn't thought about that.

If there is any one man for whom I have mighty little use it is a "Button Brother." You know who I mean. The fellow who covers the lapel of his coat with the biggest emblem he can buy of some secret order, expecting it to get him business enough to enable him to hold his job, or loans to hold him up in case he loses it. Take my tip and stay off of the "Button Brothers."

Just as soon as "positions" become "jobs" and occupation again means work—we will be getting back to normal.

My friends convinced me I was withering away like all house plants, and I would have to take up golf. Out I went to buy golf balls, sticks and bag. The first place I happened into was a hardware store, and when I came out I had a lawn mower, hoe and rake. I went home, fired the fellow I had been paying to take care of my lawn and garden, bought a set of Friend Luther Burbank's books that tell you how to make a home look like somebody lived there, and dogonit I'm feeling fine.

A successful salesman takes truth, honesty, confidence and common sense, wraps them in enthusiasm, puts them into what he has to sell, and the prospect says:--I'll take it."

Every man lives in hopes that his ideas will some day work—so he won't have to.

The great big double fisted, uneducated, ill-mannered rough neck whose father willed him a hillside farm on which oil was found is now known in Polite Society as "a He man."

The only way you will ever fit yourself for the doing of big things is by practicing the doing of little things well.

Yes, it's true, Henry Ford, Thos. Edison and Chas. M. Schwab accomplished what they have by working eight hour shifts—about two or three a day.

Much depends on what an employee has in mind doing as to whether or not it is a good idea to keep one of these "Do It Now" signs staring him in the face.

The putting of four wheel brakes on a car that is to be driven by a man or woman with a head full of loose wheels—don't mean anything.

Have you ever tried making friends of people who were not your friends just by treating them as though they were your friends?

I reckon it's because that in business they are used to figuring the worth of a concern by its liabilities that you hear so few men boasting of belonging to some church.

Undertakers are the only people in business who hear nothing but kind words spoken of everyone.

It takes so little to satisfy a self-satisfied person.

If I am ever hailed into court to prove I have a full set of brains in good working order, the first five witnesses I am going to have called, are the life insurance agents whose offices I have walked into, unsolicited and unknown, and bought insurance, just as I buy any other necessity.

Many men not only believe in dreams, but get mad when you refuse to loan money on them.

They say a growling dog seldom bites, but a growling employee has, usually, bit off more than he can chew.

When a salesman shows signs of fear, the prospect gets it as quick as a youngster catches the mumps.

Firms that periodically advertise that they are going out of business sooner or later tell the truth.

There is this to be said in favor of a hamburger steak, young onions and Welsh rarebit. If they disagree with you, you know it—they don't smile and "yes" you into thinking they agree with you—like a lot of people do.

Some salesmen forget it is repeat orders, and not repeat calls, that bring in the money to pay their salaries.

The fellow who "overlooks" things is never made an "overseer."

It is said "we live and learn," but so many people only live.

Too little wind spoils many a sail—And too much "wind" spoils many a sale.

It was on an early morning street car—she looked to be a stenographer, or telephone operator—and, carried a library book and sewing basket. I heard her say she was working down at soandso's, and the idea struck me it must be a very busy place.

I met the late Bill Smith on the street the other day. As a boy Bill was always late at school and when he grew to be a man, if he wasn't just too late to get a job, he was late often enough to lose it. He said he was a salesman for some firm and was complaining about his just having lost a nice order. I did not have to ask how the order was lost, not by the "late" Bill Smith.

The longer an argument lasts, the less part truth takes in it.

Face facts, or face failure.

A buyer don't want to believe the pessimist—can't believe the optimist—so-a salesman with a full set of brains comes along—talks sense—and—gets the order.

Honesty pays—You've heard that all your life—But, let me tell you something—If you are honest because you thinks it pays—You are not honest.

Few men ever tell you anything about their losses on horse races, poker, or through buying stock in worthless wildcat schemes; but they can give you an hour's oration on a minute's notice of their having at sometime in life loaned a fellow five or ten dollars they didn't get back, or about their having donated a few measly dollars to some worthy charity.

One time I was in a country store down in Kentucky and the old fellow who ran the place had just tacked up a card that read "terms strictly cash." A town "rounder" came in and read it aloud. The old fellow said, "the right people always see those things." I have so often thought of that when I would hear employees finding fault with some "roast" that appeared in a general letter or house organ gotten out by their firms.

It is claimed a machine has been discovered that will make a man tell the truth, but a guilty conscience will always be the one best thing to depend upon.

When you hear someone finding faults with others, you can take it from me that "others" have found out his.

When a prospective buyer tells you he will "think it over" he has told you all he is going to do—nine times out of ten.

A "satisfied employee" is quite often one who is getting more salary than he feels he is entitled to.

I believe that every employee should fill his job with dignity—and—I further believe—The harder he "digs" the longer he'll fill it.

Well read men are more often "better quoters" than thinkers.

You would think that the time to advertise, would be when the people were not buying, and business was quiet. That is what I told a merchant I was trying to sell some advertising, and he said, "Yes, and I suppose the best time to go fishing is when the fish are not biting."

I know a fellow who failed in business because the wives of men having such modest incomes as ten thousand dollars a year were so embarrassed when they approached his extravagantly dressed salesladies they quit coming to his store.

When you can look into a mud puddle and see something besides mud, and into the heart of a man and see more good than bad, you will never again be able to list

The President of our Company once said to an employee, "We are paying you too much money for what you are doing, and not enough for what you ought to be doing." Often the case.

Quite often an employee gets the idea in his head he is entitled to an increase in salary—tells his fellow employees—and they help along his imagination by agreeing with him. He thinks and talks it until he believes he has it, and starts spending it. At last he takes it up with his employer, who tells him something different—then he is in the middle of a 'ellofafix.

I expect some of you "old timers" can remember when "Where is My Wandering Boy Tonight" was a popular song. We seldom hear it now. About as near as some mothers and fathers can come to answering the question the song asks is, that he left home in his car right after dinner, and every time the phone rings they think it is the police station telling them where he is.

If a salesman won't take orders from his manager, he can't take orders from customers.

It is the fellow with a "block head" who goes around with a chip on his shoulder.

I don't mind a fellow quitting his job to show his independence, if he wouldn't come around every few days to touch me for money to live on until he can find himself another job.

No man wants a hat or suit that is far too big for him, but I have known many employees to feel they were being unjustly treated because they were not advanced to positions that were.

When you know how to spend money, you will automatically save money. Trying to save money by becoming selfish, and practicing petty stinginess will never make you a successful man.

Circus performers doing trapeze work are confident enough of success, but they prepare for a fall by stretching a net. Most men in business become so blinded by their expected success they never prepare for a fall and—

Someone has said: "It's the songs we sing and the smiles we wear, that's making the sun shine everywhere," and, take it from me, they said something.

It is easier to obey the Biblical injunction to love our enemies, if we will bear in mind that our enemies do not ask us to endorse notes, or to listen to their imaginary troubles.

We so often hear a young spendthrift referred to as being a "good spender." Such is far from being true. A good spender is one who knows the value of a dollar, and can buy a hundred cents' worth with it.

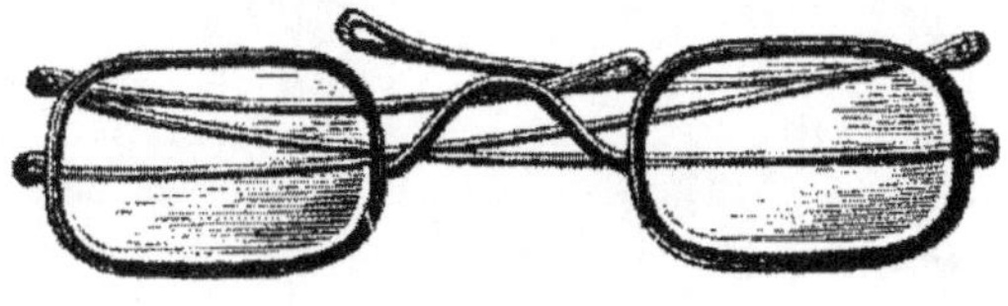

6

Believe It Or Not

Advice that is pleasing is the kind we accept—and is usually the kind we do not need.

A salesman who has become sales manager is often made general manager of a business because he not only knows what the firm has to sell, but how to sell it, who can buy it, and pay for it. These are the important things to know in the building of a successful business.

Being happy over the found out faults of others is often a confession that we have many of the same sort.

Belittle others—and be little.

Look upon your job as your business, financed by your employer, with a guaranteed profit to you, even though he takes a loss.

Others judge us by the lives we live and their verdict is our reputation, which we either live up to or live down.

When you meet a fellow who is "up against it" you will find out, that he got that way from backing up, and not by going ahead.

When a man faces his faults, the world turns its back on them.

Respect usually comes with age. As example the elderly gentlemen you hear spoken of as being eccentric, were called "nuts" or "Cracked-pots" when they were young.

When some little thing comes up that causes you to feel that you must write a nasty mean letter to a customer, do it. The quicker you get it out of your system the better off you'll be. Then when it has been written, read it, sign it, tear it up and throw it in the waste basket. This will cure you of losing your temper and your customers.

The worst that is said of those who talk about themselves is that they are conceited. The worst that is said of those who talk about others, I dare not print.

You can believe it or not; all "fakers" are not traveling with circuses and carnival companies.

We have court houses, judges, lawyers, bankruptcy courts, and poor-houses, for the convenience of those who are looking for revenge.

The success that comes from thinking is having others think as we think.

Have you ever noticed, that when one firm takes an employee away from another firm, some other firm is pretty sure to take him away from them. And have you ever noticed, that when some woman takes another woman's husband away from her—

What you think of the folks in the old home town, is just about their opinion of you.

An employee with a fiery temper is soon fired.

In our neighborhood, two men have gardens, same size, same soil, with just a fence separating them. One has cultivated his, and he has a beautiful garden. The other has not. A new neighbor moved in across the street. Both became acquainted with him at the same time. One cultivated his acquaintance, and now he has a splendid friend. The other has not. Do you get the idea?

Some banks advertise, "Make a friend of your banker." Wonder if they know there are a lot of fellows, who look upon loans made them by friends as being gifts.

The School of Experience offers but two grades—Up, and Down.

Have you ever tried being that which you think others should be?

One look at a woman who says, "In all our married life, my husband has never given me a cross word," will convince you she has a husband who uses good judgment.

You will find about as many people who think as you think, as you will those who look like you.

If shoppers would remember the "Have the exact change ready" sign on the street cars, when they are doing their buying, their troubles would be fewer on the first of each month.

Calling to mind others who are less worthy than ourselves, is sometimes easy to do, but it does not change the price tag the public has pinned on us.

It is the job of the advertising man to use his brains, in expressing what the boss thinks, in a manner that will please all salesmen, and other employees; satisfy the dealers, and incidentally sell the consumer on buying the product. Now you know why the advertising man is looked on as being the one man of the organization who has nothing at all to do.

Real men are made of what they get out of themselves, and not out of others.

A ticket collector on a merry-go-round is not the only employee who is going all the time, but getting nowhere.

Winnings are worthless if self respect is lost.

Doing a thing better than any other man has ever done it is all right, but the world will remember you longer if you will do something worth while that has not been done before.

When we are leading a clean life, very few will go ahead of us.

Have you ever noticed, that when a responsible position is to be filled, the boss seldom considers the young man who prides himself on being a "good fellow."

No sooner would a passenger finish reading a newspaper and throw it aside, than he was there to get it. I watched him take them to the rear of the car, get out some string, and tie them in packages. He excited my curiosity, and when the conductor came along, I asked him what the porter did with those papers, and he said, "He has been running on this road for years, and all along the route, he throws off papers to those who would know little of what is going on were it not for him." And then I got to questioning myself, as to how much happiness I was throwing out to others, as I traveled down the road of life. While your mind is on the subject, you might ask yourself the same question.

It is really astonishing the amount of will-power some men possess. Why, I have had hundreds of them tell me that they could quit smoking if they wanted to do so, then light another cigarette demonstrating their remarkable will-power over the quitting idea.

My kind of a man, is a kind man.

Bankers ask for interest, and so do preachers. Bankers generally get it.

If we are afraid for others to know what we are doing, we may be certain we are not doing right.

We learn to swim in smooth water, but that's not the kind of water boats usually go down in. Many a young man starting business life, tries to find an easy job, but that's not the kind of a job that offers him an opportunity to become a successful man.

It is the growling man who lives a dog's life.

It takes time to make a position out of a job. That is why nearly all worth while positions are filled with men who have been on the job a long time.

Judges of prize fights are always outside the ring. And I have found that those outside our organization can tell us a lot of things about our business that we would profit by listening to.

A secret is usually the seed of a scandal.

A sales manager who is a "goat getter" has trouble keeping salesmen who are "go getters."

I have had any number of salesmen, representing wholesale, and manufacturing concerns, offer to let me have groceries, house furnishings etc. at wholesale price, provided I would "keep it quiet" so their retail customers would not know about it. They all know what I think about such crookedness.

Unless a firm has satisfied employees, how can it ever hope to have satisfied customers?

A philanthropist is a man who enjoys the happiness of making others happy while he lives, instead of leaving what he has to a lawyer who proves he was crazy when he made his will.

Did you ever stop to think that people criticize only those they really care for or of whom they are envious or maybe jealous?

I attribute my few wrinkles at fifty-five to the fact I generally let others do the worrying about their own troubles.

"The Customer is Always Right," may be a good policy for the stores that have adopted it, but I do not believe that anyone is always right.

It all depends on whom you are talking about, whether or not I believe that ancestors were monkeys.

He had a wonderful personality, and it built for him a splendid retail business. Success assured, he spent the greater part of his time in a "hide-away" office, doing work that a fifteen dollar a week employee could have better handled. One of his clerks who came in daily contact with the patrons of the store, soon won their friendship and confidence, and it was not long until he had a store across the street, and the customers his old boss had neglected, and he had cultivated, went across the street with him.

There is always a market for trained brains.

Do any of these so-called optimists, wearing artificial smiles, ever rush in to see you, right when you are as busy as can be in trying to figure out some important business problems, give you the "glad-hand," then start telling you that everybody's happy—there is no such thing as worry—business is booming—prosperity is assured, and wind up wanting to borrow five dollars? That is another reason why I think every business man should keep a loaded gun in the top drawer of his desk for quick use.

All men are born equal, but they soon start making the necessary changes, that the pulpits and prisons may be filled.

So many salesmen credit themselves with having enthusiasm, when they are but overly excited at the prospect of making a worth while sale.

When anyone leads off with, "If I were you, I'd do this—" right then I quit listening, for I know that nothing more than a lot of unasked for, worthless advice is going to be unloaded at my door.

Keep your business out of your religion, by putting your religion into your business.

Advancing an employee to a responsible position, which carries a high sounding title, without giving him sufficient increase in salary to meet the social and business demands of the position, often means the nominating of another candidate for the penitentiary.

I suppose the reason we look upon a book as a good friend is because we can depend upon its telling us tomorrow exactly the same story that it tells us to-day.

The bone of contention is usually a "bone-head."

After adding the small bill twice, he had it added on the adding machine to make sure it was right. Then he took a party of six of us to lunch, and when the waiter presented the check to him he glanced at the total, and accepted the waiter's addition without question.

Look upon your mind as a garden, in which to plant thoughts, to grow into worth-while things. And remember, all gardens need weeding now and then.

As we entered his home, he was telling me how he managed the twelve hundred men he had working for him. Then a ninety pound wife, and a three year old youngster showed me how they managed him.

I count mighty little on education without inspiration, backed up with a lot of determination.

If with your acquaintances you can inspire confidence, you will build friendships that will make it easier to answer, "How's business?"

When a salesman lets some subordinate in the outer office turn him down, he loses nothing for the buyer would have likely done as much had he succeeded in getting in to see him.

Few have time to stop and pet every barking dog.

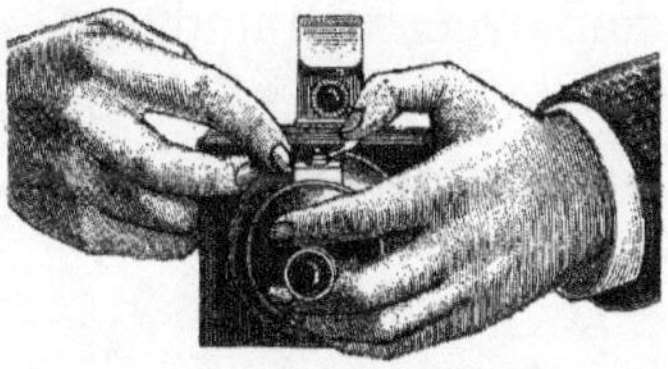

When only your banker can appraise your worth, you are a poor man.

We make our own friends, and enemies.

It is alright to have your heart in your work, but use your head too.

Captains of industry are not hunting money, they are seeking brains—specialized brains—and faithful, loyal service.

Because we think differently, therefore live, dress and act differently, I look just as wrong to you, as you do to me. But, why criticize, when the chances are, neither of us is right.

The first fellow to remove his hat in a public elevator is the young man with a "permanent wave" or well vaselined hair, and the things the baldheaded men think about him, more than offset what the ladies might think.

So long as your habits and morals are not ragged, you need not worry much about your clothes.

Whether you believe "Mind is all" or not, you will have to confess that the man who minds his own business, and makes his youngsters mind him, has some ideas worth copying.

It might not be a bad idea for a salesman to send in only such orders as he would fill, if he owned the business.

If honest enough to face the truth, ninety-eight percent of discharged employees will find that either laziness, disloyalty, conceit, untruthfulness, dishonesty, trouble making, or talking too much got them their walking-papers.

Another good way to be happy is to look upon that which you have as being the best, inasmuch as it is the best you have.

If a salesman has not the respect, confidence and friendship of those inside his own organization, with whom he is in daily contact, he is not going to enjoy such on the outside.

What you are, is the result of what you were.

The only thing a heated argument ever produced, is a coolness.

Whether or not an employee is receiving "a living wage," depends entirely on whether or not he is willing to live according to his earning capacity.

If there is any one thing in life I don't want to be, it is a detective, giving my life to looking for bad in men, in the place of good. Looking not for the smiles on faces, but for faces on which there are prices in the form of rewards.

I am wondering if the reason boys are not what they used to be, when we were boys, and employees do not work like we did, when we were employees, can be accounted for by our having had better fathers and better employers.

A spider kept putting up web after web in our basement, as fast as I would tear them down. He taught me that, by using the same sort of persistency, I could be a better salesman.

Lives of great men oft remind us—how far from great we are.

Going out of your way, often causes things to come your way.

Inasmuch as the all important thing in business is Getting the business, it has often occurred to me, that if the small neighborhood merchant would take an hour from his store each day, and personally call on those not doing business with him, he would secure at least one customer a day and by rendering them the service promised the time would not be long when he would have a real business. People like to personally know those they are doing business with.

One of the first things to learn in selling, to save your firm a lot of money, and yourself your job, is that, "I will take it up with the board," "You might drop in later on," and "I will let you hear from me," all mean—NO.

Years of sampling the "home cooking" advertised by restaurants has made many men bachelors.

The fellow that moves in the right circle, is usually on the square.

A successful merchant was telling me he always penciled the name of a new customer, and then put it somewhere on his desk, where he would handle it several times a day and by this simple system he was not only able to address all new customers by name, but enjoyed the reputation of having a most remarkable memory.

Do as best you can, that which you are supposed to do, and soon you will have something better to do.

When you lose control of your car, you are pretty sure to have a wreck on your hands. P. S. Read that again, substituting the word "son" for car.

There are just so many customers, and the only way your competitor can increase his business is by taking yours from you.

The fellow who does not credit himself with knowing it all, is the man every employer is looking for

It was Saturday afternoon. I was alone in my office. A man walked in and said, "I am here to see Mr. Lewis." I answered, "As you of course know; there is no such man here." He said, "Well then I must have the wrong address. Mr. Lewis phoned me to call this afternoon and explain a new policy our company is writing. Inasmuch as I will not be able to see him, I wonder if you could give me five minutes." I answered, I would be delighted to do so. When he was seated, I said in part, (the printable part) "I am going to give you five minutes, all of which I am going to use myself, in trying to stop you from going around making a 'darn fool' of yourself, in looking upon others as being that which you are. I look upon the life insurance business as being more than a business. It is a lifetime necessity, and a blessing afterwards. And, it makes me as mad as a wet hen to have a fellow like you disgracing it. Business is founded on confidence. You destroyed all confidence I might have had in you and your company by attempting that old time worn trick approach. You have had the promised five minutes, and I will ask that you close the door from the outside."

If one's interest in life is so weak that he hopes some day to be able to live without work, he is headed for failure, no matter how successful he may be in the hoarding of money.

Be Charitable, but start by granting to others the right to live their lives the way they wish to live them and don't forget they are generally conceding to you that same right.

Many aspire to become writers. If you have any thoughts along those lines, start by seeing how long a story you can write under this head, "What have I ever done that has made this world better?"

You are getting the best of a man, in the winning of his confidence.

A dressmaker had been in for the day, and seeing the floor covered with pins, I said to my wife, "Why don't that dressmaker pick up the pins she drops?" Mrs. Cox answered, "Why, Coleman, a dressmaker's time is worth too much to her to be picking up pins." Then I called to mind a lot of "picking up pins" I had been doing during the day, by giving my time to work that the office boy could have easily done.

Believe about half you hear, though be sure it is the right half.

Can a man lose something he never had? The reason I am asking, we so often hear salesmen telling about the fine sales they "lost."

In trying to "sell" me on playing golf, a friend of mine was telling me that there is no better place to talk business to a man than on a golf course. That settled it. Now I know golf is no game for me. I would never want to trust myself out in a quiet secluded place with a club in my hand, talking business to some of those with whom I have come in contact.

The worst pests I have to contend with are my very closest friends who upon every occasion bore me to extinction in trying to convince me that I should give up all things of life that mean pleasure and happiness to me, and live my life as they are living theirs.

Nearly any street car we take in San Francisco will get us to the Ferry Building. No waiting friend questions, or cares, which car carried us. When I hear people having a religious argument, I cannot but think of the Ferry cars, and of how little it matters which route we travel, just so long as we get where we hope to go, and join our waiting loved ones.

Grasping an opportunity amounts to mighty little, unless you can grasp a pen and write a check that will enable you to take advantage of it.

Many who seek the company of others, find that being alone with their thoughts is too great a punishment.

When manufacturers get wise, and start selling the salesmen, who sell the consumer, the buyer will have to buy. And besides that, the salesmen of today are going to be the merchants of tomorrow.

The fellow who lies abed longest in the morning, has the best start on lying for the day.

We have all seen the fellow who stands between capital and labor—because he stands on a soap box.

Whether or not money buys happiness, depends entirely upon what it takes to make us happy. Sometimes a comfortable home, an automobile, good clothes, or possibly travel to make people happy, and they all cost money.

It is a right good idea to figure the time your sales letter and advertising matter will reach its destination; remembering that waste baskets do an over-flow business Saturdays and Mondays.

If we could make a great bonfire of the thousands of laws we have in this country, and start all over again with only the Golden Rule, and the Ten Commandments, I am sure we would get along much better.

Just so long as you keep on asking people how they are feeling, they are going to keep on telling you. So you have nobody to blame but yourself.

If you feel you must tell the faults of someone, then tell your own. You will not only have more to talk about, but can easily confine yourself to the truth.

Only those who are "easy" invest in schemes promising easy money.

When friends of other days commence their "I knew him when" talk, and competitors start knocking their darndest, you've arrived.

In no home, hotel or cafe, has food ever been so well prepared, but that one occasionally becomes tired of it, and wants a change. Just so it is with food for thought, given salesmen by sales managers. Speaking as a salesman with thirty-five years' experience in selling, I believe that the best organization that could be formed to improve salesmen and thereby improve business, would be one composed of sales managers of different organizations, to exchange visits and give talks to salesmen at weekly sales meetings. Enthusiasm is the secret of success in selling.

Failure will never knock at the door of a man who can truthfully say, "I am honest, fair and square in all my dealings with others. I am honest with myself."

When packing your grip to attend a sales conference it is just as well you leave out your alibis, and imaginary troubles, that no one is at all interested in, and bring along a few new ideas that can be used to an advantage by the other boys.

There isn't anything on earth that an honest man need be afraid of.

Give all of your sympathy to those who are without friends.

We all have our troubles. Employers fire theirs. Employees quit theirs. Kindly judges divorce others of theirs.

A friend was telling me of a merchant that sent a wholesaler quite an order and immediately received a telegram that read, "We cannot fill your order until you have paid your long overdue account." To which the merchant replied as follows, "Cancel the order. Cannot wait that long."

Salesmen of the higher type, representing firms of high standing, that market merchandise of high quality, never resort to high pressure sales tactics.

The fellow who is always ready to oppose anything suggested, truthfully starts off with, "I don't think."

When a merchant uses up his time and my time in trying to sell me something that's "just as good," in the place of giving me what I ask for, and want, I always find another store that's just as good.

If there is one single thing that can wreck a perfectly happy home, it is an uninvited guest, who moves in bag and baggage, and stays until everyone in the house is a bunch of nerves.

What you are depends on what you think, but that does not mean all men are what they think they are.

About the only good luck I have ever had has been a willingness to work.

All men have at some time in life attained success, but a record is only kept of those that retained it.

In trying to sell me on making an aeroplane trip he said, "Coleman, you'll never know a real thrill until you've been up in the air." Then I told him of a prospect who had me "up in the air" for nearly three years and one day when my hope of selling him registered about three degrees below zero, I made a drop-in call on him, such having become a sort of a habit with me. To my astonishment he wore a friendly smile and before I could speak he said, "I'm ready to sign that contract this morning." After that experience, I am sure the aeroplane has no thrills for me.

It is easy enough to know the right way to do a thing because all other ways are wrong.

At railroad crossings is not the only place we see wrecks, because of people having failed to stop, look, and listen.

The Pacific Coast manager of a very large Eastern concern was telling me there were no good salesmen to be had. When he told me the salaries they paid, I agreed with him.

A salesman who used to work for us in reporting on a prospect said, "I wish you could have heard his objections. Why, before I got through with him, he felt like crawling in a rat hole." I answered, "But, you did not get his order. You have but lost a good prospect. No salesman can get an order from the man he causes to feel he would like to crawl in a rat hole."

There is one man you and I will never live long enough to forget. He is the fellow who came to us the morning we tackled our first job, put his hand on our shoulder, and with a smile, said in the friendliest sort of a way, "My boy, you are getting along fine. Take it easy, don't get worried, and if you need any help, just call on me."

This dealer Good Will that we hear so much about is nothing more than the Confidence and Friendship of the buying public a merchant enjoys, because of his having given more thought to the wants of his customers than his wanting to get their money in his till.

I credit the small percentage of failures we have in business to the fact, that few men ever try out the advice they offer others, and they use good judgment in not doing it.

I suppose my being quick to excuse others of their mistakes, comes from the great amount of practice I have in excusing my own.

The best proof I have to offer, that I know something about selling, is the fact that the credit man of the firm I have been with for fifteen years, is the best friend I have.

We used to have a rather large card framed and hanging in our sales room that read, "Time not spent in the presence of a prospective buyer is time lost." There's a lot of truth in that.

A friend of mine who has two sons, gave each of them fifty cents. One of them bought a copy of a worth while magazine for a dime, and spent the evening at home reading it. The next morning, he had more sense in his head, and more cents in his pocket. The other spent his half dollar on a picture show. I am offering a hundred to one odds, and taking all bets offered on the first boy.

Service, is a much abused word. If you want to know the real meaning of it, you have but to stop at an oil station, and buy a few gallons of gasoline.

A concession not only creates doubt in the mind of the buyer, but destroys confidence in the salesmen, and the firm he represents.

Babe Ruth is hired to make home runs. Salesmen are hired to make sales. I have known sales managers to yell themselves hoarse, in showing Babe their appreciation of his efforts. The appreciation shown him for the making of one home run, caused him to want to go right out and make another. Now you have the idea, that's all.

To say a man is a good driver does not necessarily mean he is a golfer or a motorist. Maybe he's an employer.

"At an early hour this morning," is one line of type newspapers keep standing to print stories of young people being killed or crippled in automobile accidents.

Your credit being good means nothing to your grocer or butcher, unless you pay your bills so they can pay theirs. A butcher who has a stand in a neighborhood market was telling me about a very wealthy woman who owed him a three months bill. He asked her for the money and she paid him, saying, "I'd have you know my credit is good. I have been in your place my last time, for I am not in the habit of having such people as butchers ask me for money." Can you beat it?

Once upon a time ladies thought that smoking ruined lace curtains.

Many men are credited with being dignified when they are nothing more than self-conscious to the point of being afraid to say anything.

Sometime ago I had the pleasure of visiting my good friend Mr. Thos. A. Edison, and he was telling me that by leaving it to ministers and politicians, to talk religion and politics, he had saved a lot of time to give matters he knew more about. A good idea.

When enthusiasm is inspired by reason; controlled by caution; sound in theory; practical in application; reflects confidence; spreads good cheer; raises morale; inspires associates; arouses loyalty, and laughs at adversity, it is beyond price.

The lambs that gambol get fleeced. Men who gamble, sooner or later have the same experience.

There are few business men in San Francisco who do not know Tommy. Five per cent of them have never even seen Edward. Tommy goes from dining room to dining room, selling cigars. Edward is the manager of the hotel, at a very large salary, and enjoys the reputation of being one of the best known hotel men in America. When I hear a fellow boasting about being known by everyone, I think of Tommy. Then I think of Edward.

It has been said that nothing has ever been made so good but what some impostor could make it worse and sell it for less.

There is no place in the business world for the young man, who in applying for a position says, "I'm willing to do anything." That is but a confession he cannot do anything. Positions are filled with men who can do some one thing, and do it well. Real success comes to those who can do it better than it has ever been done.

The office clock may not lose time, but those that watch it do.

What I would call a "good looking" man, is one who has lived a life so clean, his thoughts have stamped their impressions upon his countenance.

After it is all over, then we start receiving callers from the "I told you so," and "You wouldn't listen to me" branches of the Prattle Club, no member of which ever told anyone a dime's worth about anything.

A friend of mine, who had proved himself a successful sales manager, learned that the manufacturer of a nationally known washing machine was in San Francisco, looking for a suitable man to fill the position of Pacific Coast sales manager, and applied for the job. The manufacturer said that while there was no doubt but what he was an A-1 sales manager, he could not consider his application because he did not know the washing machine business. When he told me that, I said, "You go right back and tell him, that it might be easier to teach a sales manager how to make washing machines than it would be to teach a washing machine man how to makes sales." He did, and got the job.

Be charitable, and do not be too quick in criticizing those who talk too much. Remember they are men who think little things, and therefore have more to talk about than men who think big things.

The only things one merchant has to offer a customer that he can't get at some other store, is his smile, his hand—in other words his personality.

Have you ever noticed that young couples starting married life, who go far enough away to rid themselves of their 'in-laws and other advising relatives, usually get along very well?

"How are they coming?" is a greeting that should never be used, on meeting a friend, who has mortgaged his life for years to come by buying everything offered him on the monthly "easy to pay" plan.

Some years ago I saw a poker game in Butte, Montana, where the chips represented one, two and five hundred dollars each. When the game was over they were not worth two cents. Then I have seen isolated swamp lands divided into fifty foot lots, and sold at several thousand dollars each while the boom was on; after which—

The art of getting things done, is mostly a matter of concentration, and rapid elimination of non-essentials.

Business is not always rushing with firms who advertise "Your Credit Is Good" because those reading their ads know different.

Never ask a hotel man how many towels and pieces of silverware are carried away by guests, if you want to keep on thinking everybody is honest.

A friend was telling me that he headed his list of wasters of time and money, with the names of four life insurance companies, who mailed him cards every birthday, telling him how happy they were that he was living, and expressing their hope that he would always continue to do so.

I have found that by being pleasant with others and not making cutting remarks, that hurt and humiliate them without profiting me in the least, is a mighty good way to make and hold friends.

When a man is happy in his home he is happy in his work and happiness is the pathway to success.

Before you change jobs or towns, to better your condition, suppose you try changing your mental attitude, habits and associates, then go to work, and work harder than you have ever worked before. If these changes fail to bring about the desired results, you may be sure that you would have been a failure in any other town, and at any other job you might have tackled.

I had made up my mind to shake from my feet the dust of the little Kentucky town in which I was raised. I was to leave for far away California in search of fame and fortune. In going around to tell my friends goodbye, I saw my old friend Max Gundlefinger standing out in front of his little clothing store. I crossed the street to say goodbye and Max said: "Coleman I think you are making a great mistake, but I do not suppose there is any need of my saying anything to you, since you have fully made up your mind to go, but I do want to give you a little piece of advice, and I want you to promise me you will always remember it wherever you may go." I assured him I would, and placing both hands on my shoulders he said: "People who live in glass houses gather no moss." Thirty-five years have passed since then, and I am still keeping the promise made Max. It is not what you say, but how you say it that makes a lasting impression.

A stranger has no other way of judging whether we are going ahead, standing still, or backing up, except by the looks of things around our places of business. Dilapidated fixtures, antique desks and rickety chairs give no one the impression that we are doing business in an up-to-date way.

The salesman who starts with, "I want to tell you a good one on a Scotchman"—usually gets a laugh. The one who starts with, "I want to tell you how you can make more money"—usually gets an order.

The best piece of advice offered you in this booklet is printed on the cover, and at the top of each page.

Get rich quick schemes, and men who get good quick, have never appealed to me.

It takes training to make a winner of a thoroughbred horse. When I see so many young men from fine families failing to make good in the world I wonder if such failures are not due to lack of training.

Before you worry about something you want, look around at the things you have, about which you worried a great deal until you got them, but now regard so lightly.

A Convention is the bringing together of several hundred men who are engaged in the same line of business—and play golf.

While the orchestra is playing the overture the performers are getting ready to put on the show. While some salesmen are talking their first five or ten minutes, they are trying to think of something to say.

My first sales experience was with a very large concern. I was quite successful considering my youth and lack of experience. The success I was enjoying, soon developed for me about the best bump of ego that any young man ever had. My fellow employees amused themselves in encouraging me in my conceited belief, that the firm would have a mighty hard time getting along without me and that every competitor was just waiting his chance to grab me. One day I decided that the time had come, when I should give the firm a chance to decide whether they should increase my salary and remain in business or refuse me and go broke. The latter idea appealed to them so much they decided that my leaving them should take place immediately. For three months I walked the streets looking for a job. The lesson was worth it.

Nearly all luncheon clubs start their meetings with the singing of the Star Spangled Banner or America. That is done to prove to each of those present, that he is not the only man who can't sing, and does not know the words of either song, which creates more of a brotherly feeling.

During my thirty-five years in selling I have not used a hundred business cards. For years I have never carried one. My experience has been, that when the card goes in to the office of an executive of a large concern, the salesman seldom does. And I have never known a card to bring out a signed order.

No story of Success ever starts with "if" and "but."

I stept inside a retail store, and started talking advertising to the merchant. He said, "I am through with advertising. No one reads it. You never see a man reading a car card, billboard or newspaper ad. All we use are these fine windows of ours." Just then I said aloud—" Ninety-One." He asked what I meant, and I answered, "While you were talking, I was counting the people passing your windows, and not one out of ninety-one turned a head to look at them. Why don't you quit them too?"

Only those who see the "Keep to the Right" and "No Parking" signs along the road to success, ever get anywhere.

The salesman who takes "no" for an answer from prospective buyers, gets "no" for an answer, when he asks for an increase in salary or a promotion.

Success in life comes with the substitution of information for imagination.

The knowledge and ability to perform useful honest labor of any kind is infinitely important and of more value than all the so-called culture.

I saw a wonderful letter that a large manufacturing concern mailed its customers, telling of the passing of one of their employees, the closing lines of which read, "In forty years Steve Enright never failed us in truth, in honesty, in friendship, in loyalty, or in duty," I have been trying to call to mind another Steve Enright.

He was a tall lanky Southerner, a droll talker, with a very pronounced Southern accent. Years ago he and I worked together on several Eastern newspapers. Sometime ago I was surprised to meet him in San Francisco. When he told me he had quit the newspaper business and was now "entertaining" I laughed heartily. He said, "That's it, Coxey. It's the laughingest darn business a fellow was ever in. My friends all laugh when I tell them about it. I go out and talk at some luncheon or banquet, and everybody laughs and laughs and laughs. Then they give me a check—and I go home and laugh and laugh and laugh."

Even the woodpecker owes his success to the fact he uses his head and keeps pecking away until he finishes the job he starts.

He was a salesman, and was elevated to the position of sales manager. In little or no time his memory went ninety per cent bad on him. All he could remember was the one out of ten prospects he sold. The other nine, he had forgotten.

When a goat starts backing-up, he is getting ready to do something. When a salesman starts backing-up—he is about through.

The young man starting life with a charge account, seldom opens a savings account.

Few men are either as good or as bad, as their friends and enemies would have us believe they are.

It is just as easy for me to believe some writers and speakers, who contend that any man can become a successful salesman, as it is for me to think that it is all my own fault that I cannot sing as Caruso sang, or paint the pictures Rembrandt did.

Many a man's happy recollection of the old swimming pool has been forever ruined by his taking a trip to see it after many years and finding it a part of an irrigation ditch.

Since people are known by the company they keep, it is a good plan to ask ourselves occasionally, whether we are elevating our associates any in the minds of the people.

Have you ever seen a bird taking a look at nests it built in other years, that it might build a better one this year? Neither have I. And I have always figured that a better way of beating last year's sales records this year, was to get out and sell more merchandise, and waste less time figuring out past records, that are worth little more, than a last year's bird's nest.

He was one of the kind that is always looking for someone to be sorry for him, and when I saw him approaching, I took on the most dejected look possible. In his usual pathetic voice, he asked me my trouble. I assured him there was nothing the matter with me. That I was only prepared to be sorry for him.

We suffer less from being "bit," than we do from the nervousness brought on by fleas and fidgety salesmen who jump around from place to place while they work on us.

Offending does not breed Befriending.

I have often wondered how hotel men could call all guests by names. After hearing some of their unjust complaints, I have wondered how the hotel men could resist calling them a lot of names.

Yes, I have tried many "trick approaches" in selling, but inasmuch as none of them ever got me any business, why tell them.

When you buy friends with anything other than friendship, they do not stay bought long.

The experiences, observations and passing thoughts contained in this little book, were written with a smile, and I hope you have worn one while reading them. The smiling away of our own little worries, and helping others smile away theirs, makes life so much more enjoyable. If I have made you happier, then I am happier.

7 Just As I Thought

There are many ways of making good in life, but those who try the most of them are almost certain to become failures.

Every man will drop any grudge he may be carrying if you will hit him with kindness.

We all believe in luck, when we hear about the success of someone we dislike.

If an employee works hard eight hours a day, he will hold his job and have nothing to worry about. As a further reward, maybe he will be made manager of the business, then he can work fourteen to twenty hours a day, and worry himself to death.

When you are looking for the best of it, you are but trying to give some other fellow the worst of it.

I never see a person who is without troubles, because I never look at a corpse.

Many employees live in hope that they will some day be worth $50,000. And so do their employers, since the three thousand dollars a year that they are paying them is six per cent on a $50,000.00 investment.

When the neighbors drop in to spend the evening, we either cause them to feel at home, or wish they were there.

The big reason many salesmen are not convincing talkers is because neither they nor the prospective buyer believe what they are saying.

It would be an easy matter to "do unto others as we would have them do unto us" if we did not have to watch them so closely to see that they did not do unto us, something we would not do unto them.

Peace of mind comes only to him who has nothing for which he should apologize.

Talk may be cheap, but too much talk has cost many a man his job.

About all a dog does is eat, drink, sleep and play. When a middle age man retires from business, about all he does is eat, drink, sleep and play. I have no desire whatever to live a dog's life.

When we try to do business with our personal friends, we usually lose their friendship. When we make personal friends of our business friends we usually lose their business.

The fellow who says, "When I make up my mind, that settles it," is boasting of the accomplishing of a mighty small undertaking.

A real salesman looks upon every man as being a live prospect.

I was applying for a position as salesman. The manager said, "Well I do not know where we could put you, for we have neither office or desk room for you." I answered, "You have evidently misunderstood me. I am not an office worker. I am a salesman. I expect to spend my time in the office of prospective buyers, and they will sign their contracts on their own desks." I got the job.

No man can make a fool of me. That's my specialty.

Plan to have some gold in your pocket, when you have silver in your hair.

When traveling I am frequently asked, "Is this a business trip, or a pleasure trip," I truthfully answer, "If business is good, it will be a pleasure trip."

Now is the time to do anything that really ought to be done, and NEVER will be plenty soon enough to do the questionable thing.

Are you working with the construction crew, or the wrecking gang?

Before coining some fool name for a business or product it might be well to call to mind the best known hats, shoes, clothing, automobiles and food products, all of which carry the names of their makers.

If you think life is a funny proposition, just try laughing your banker out of paying an overdue note.

It is all right for you to "take your time," but be careful that in so doing you are not taking the time of others, which may be worth something.

I expect you see some fellow every day who needs a good talking to. I know I do. And I see him while I am shaving.

To wish a young man success and happiness when his father has selected his life's occupation and his mother has chosen his wife, is placing entirely too much faith in wishing.

Hard work is the only cure for failure.

Keep company with such persons as you would be willing to introduce to your mother, should that opportunity present itself. Those that this rule would force you to overlook will not cause you any great loss.

The most expensive mistake made by business concerns is taking their best producing salesmen out of selling and giving them office work as promotions, rather than give them an increase in salary, and keep them busy bringing in the business. Keep producers producing, and keep them happy by paying them real money for that which they produce, and watch your profits increase. Some of the best sales managers I have worked for or known could not go out and hold up their end along with ordinary salesmen, but they knew who could buy, and whether or not they could pay their bills. These are the things a salesman wants to know.

What a great old world this would be if Truth and Honesty were as well advertised as cigarettes, chewing gum and laundry soaps.

A successful business enterprise is such because a man or woman had an ideal and worked unceasingly to make it a reality. That same ideal would have never been a reality without honest work; untiring, intelligently applied energy and co-operation of all employees and associates.

We have the satisfaction of knowing that the bee that stings us is going to die almost immediately, but when some "sure-thing" salesman stings us, all we can do is hope.

One of my happiest friends tells me that he is always happy because he has everything he wants; that he has everything he wants, because he never wants anything he knows he can't have.

I have had several executive jobs wished upon me but I have never been happier than when I was a salesman going about making friends for my firm and myself, and incidentally making money for my customers, my firm and myself. That has meant far more to me than a swivel-chair and a high sounding title.

Few of us remember those who have done us favors, but no man ever forgets the fellow who turned him down.

A great many people are attending church these days because they enjoy the novelty of going into a house where they are not asked to drink some sort of concoction that is by courtesy described as a cocktail or a gin fizz.

While I have never been on an operating table, I have worked for some men who could "take the heart out of me" in two minutes and kill all the enthusiasm I had with which to start a day's work.

Anyone can find fault, and those who find the most, have the most.

He is an elderly gentleman, and has been quite successful in business. He is the happy type of a fellow one is always glad to meet. We met at the theatre, and when I asked him how he was enjoying the show he answered: "I think it's fine. All of my life I have made it a rule to see several shows a week. I always come to the theatre expecting to see a good show, and I always do." Then I got to thinking that maybe he started each day expecting it to be a happy and successful one, and they had mostly been just what he expected them to be.

You can take a train and go where you want to go. But you are going to have to train yourself, to become that which you want to be.

When a salesman commences finding fault with that which he is selling, its price, or his territory, he is confessing his inability to sell, and his employer would do well to start looking for another man for his place.

It is the taking of interest that keeps banks going. And the members of service clubs, lodges and other organizations might profit by this truth.

If said about us, it is accepted as a compliment. If said about someone we are not particularly fond of, we look upon it as being nothing but flattery.

A failure may talk for hours on "what ought to be done" but you will profit more by listening to a successful man talk five minutes about what has been done.

Some of these days radio advertisers are going to find out that more people are talked out of buying, than are ever talked into buying.

Our leading men are followers of a principle.

Nothing truer was ever said than: "I used to tell my troubles to everyone I knew, and the more I told my troubles, the more my troubles grew."

One day I was visiting Mr. Thos. A. Edison, and I remarked that I came East to address a number of clubs and business organizations. He said, "I suppose I enjoy after-dinner talks more than any man living. Because of my deafness, I cannot hear anything the speaker is saying, and no one can say anything to me, because they would have to talk so loud that it would break up the meeting. I make good use of the time in figuring out what I am going to do when I get back to the laboratory."

Quit worrying about what other people are thinking about you. They do not know as much about your cussedness as you do, and therefore they are not thinking that which you know they have a right to think about you.

Maybe we would get along better were it not that we under-estimate the value of the thoughts of others, and over-estimate the worth of our own.

Many salesmen have great confidence in themselves, and wonder why they are unable to win the confidence of others. What they really have is an over developed case of egotism which does not inspire confidence.

B. C. Forbes once asked John D. Rockefeller to what he attributed his business success. He replied "to others." Every man can say as much. That does not mean that we are deprived of the credit of becoming failures because of our own mistakes, bad judgment and laziness.

We all believe that every man deserves all he gets—provided we get what we want, and those we don't care much about get what we think is coming to them.

Just how long a business can "carry on" depends upon the kind of employees they carry on their payroll.

In the place of agreeing with those who are thinking that this old world of ours is going from bad to worse, and that a large part of its population is made up of murderers and criminals of all sorts, I had rather think that the facilities for transmitting the kind of news that they like to read have been greatly improved.

What you do depends upon what you are. What you are depends upon what you think. There is no such thing possible as going wrong if you are thinking right.

The man to sell is the man you have sold. Keep on selling him and you will not only hold and increase his business, but he will sell others for you. I have been credited with making many sales, when all I did was take the order, or write the contract. The sale was made by those I had sold, and kept sold. While all firms want, and must have new business, at the same time neglecting old business to get new business is mighty poor business. Business is founded upon confidence and friendship, and we cannot make a man a customer of ours without having won both. Nor can we afford to lose either by neglecting him to go after new business, for every repeat order, or renewed contract, is worth two new ones. I have known salesmen to spend weeks and months in winning the friendship and confidence of a buyer, and when they had his name on the dotted line the buyer had seen the last of them.

It is the profit on re-orders that pay the dividends.

Never try to convince the fellow who tries to tell the boss how to run his business, that there is no such thing as "hard-luck."

More young men are wishing for the physique of a pugilist, than for the brain of an Edison, a Burbank or a Caesar.

Matrimony is the world's best cure for egotism.

Efficiency is nothing more than a "highbrow" name for the use of common-sense in business.

The Know Nothing class is largely made up of those who listen and read to find fault instead of listening and reading to learn.

I suppose it is all in the way we look at it, but the so-called "tipping evil" has always been looked upon by me as a real pleasure. It offers me an opportunity to show my appreciation of service rendered. If the tipping of hotel and Pullman employees were not permitted, then I would have the amount of my tips added to my bill, or the cost of my ticket. As the matter now stands my piece of silver gets me better service, an appreciative smile and an "I thank you" that gives me the feeling that I have made others happy, and that makes me happier.

I think that husbands should take their wives to their golf clubs. Then I think there are some wives who should take their golf clubs to their husbands.

Every successful firm has a well worked out sales policy, and they have a perfect right to expect all salesmen to live up to that policy. There is no doubt that many new salesmen have better ideas as to the way the business should be run than has the boss himself, but inasmuch as the firm has made its own plans I don't know but it would be just as well to let things go on the way the firm has planned they should go. What a firm wants of an employee, more than complaint or advice about the business, is cooperation and honest effort to do that which he is employed to do, and do it in the way employers want it done. The better it is done, the bigger the salary check and the more likely the employee is to be advanced to a better position.

I have always worried, and I always hope to do so, because my worries can usually be traced to my own faults, and the penalty that worry inflicts upon me means the correction of them.

Many mothers live in hope that their sons will never have any of the traits of their fathers, and that their daughters will not make the mistakes they did in the selecting of husbands.

The best salesmen I have met were neither too short nor too tall; over weight nor under weight, optimists nor pessimists, fluent talkers nor overly silent, lavishly dressed nor poorly dressed. They were just ordinary men who knew their business, loved their business, and WORKED.

Those who boast the most about the accomplishments of their ancestors confess that personally they have done nothing worth talking about.

When liquor, education or a sudden streak of prosperity commences to go to a fellow's head, he is all ready to show you what a complete fool a man can make of himself.

Every once in a while some one tries to tell me that the youth of this day are headed for ruin. Maybe so, but when I was a youth I heard the same thing.

We all want what is coming to us and when we do not get it there is trouble in sight. When a firm employs a salesman, it does so because he has convinced them that he can go out and get business, and the firm has a right to expect what is due them for the salary they are paying. When the employer tells the salesman that if he does bring in the business he is to receive an increase in pay, and perhaps a promotion to a better territory, the salesman expects it. He is entitled to it and should have it. It is not getting what is coming to us that causes a lot of trouble between employer and employee.

Never mind about your cash being low — how's your Character?

It takes hazards and hindrances to make golf interesting and that is equally true of business; yes, life in general.

I knew a firm who advertised, "Every customer is a satisfied customer" and in that they were right. Nearly every customer was "satisfied" that one trip to their store was enough, and it was not long until the sheriff decorated their door with a padlock.

First comes Character, then Achievement, then Success.

The idea some employees have as to the increasing of sales are about as original as telegrams to radio stations that read, "program coming in fine."

Make a business, and make money, but do not neglect the making of friends too, because their memory of you is all that will live, when you are gone.

To a man who knows nothing of football technique, the most complicated plays mean nothing. And the same goes for the business recruit, who can see no sense in an antiquated policy upon which a very wonderful business has been built.

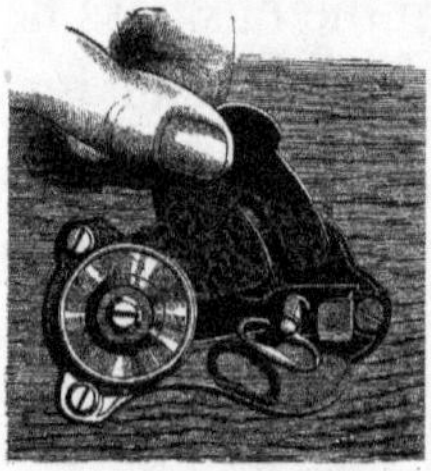

The phonograph, the flying machine and the great Bush Terminals were once but thoughts in the minds of Edison, Wright and Irving T. Bush. We would not have one of them today had their sponsors have listened to that popular song of the failures, "it can't be done."

Pray—why certainly. But salesmen who bring in the most orders close their prayers pretty much the same as the old preacher who said, "Lord if you can't send me a Christmas turkey, then please send me where there is one."

Too much self respect, and not enough respect for your employer, your fellow employees and your job, entitles you to a "good-bye" check.

We are living in a machine age. Business, however, always has been and always will be man-made. Of course some plan must be followed in the building of a business, but when a business is so thoroughly systematized that it is no longer human it is bound to fail. Looking upon employees as mere cogs in a wheel operated to grind out business is all wrong. The success of the Bethlehem Steel Company is due far more to its having been humanized by Charles M. Schwab than to its having been systematized by a lot of efficiency experts.

Farmers do not loan or give away their acreage, nor do machinists, barbers or carpenters like to loan or give away their tools, which they themselves need use of in earning a living. Perhaps that is why men who have dollars that they must keep working to earn them a living do not like to loan or give them away.

If the prospective buyer were to ever think of one tenth of the excuses for not buying that the salesman calling on him is expecting him to offer, there would never be a sale made.

Remember that nature gave you two ears with which to hear, and one tongue—that you may not repeat more than half of it.

I had a friend who for many years worked for a man in St. Louis that had the reputation of being just about the meanest man that ever stood in shoe-leather. My friend heard of a better position with another firm and applied for it. The manager asked, "What kind of a man is Mr. Crawford to work for?" My friend answered, "He is the best man I ever knew, or worked for, and I am going to regret leaving him very much." The manager looked at him in astonishment and said, "You have the job. Any man who can speak a good word for that old reprobate will at least have kindly words to say about us, should you ever quit this job." Do you get the idea?

Down in Old Kentucky where I was born and raised, they used to say that no man could eat a quail a day for thirty days. I don't know whether there is any truth in that or not. But I will say this, that in years that followed and after I had worked for a number of sales managers, it looked an easy thing to do. Sales letters are supposed to be food for thought, and after I had been fed one or more a day for months and months, my digestive apparatus went back on me. I believe in sales letters, bulletins and house-organs when rightly used, but they are often abused.

The average business man can easily keep a secret by putting it in writing, for neither he nor any other living mortal would ever be able to read it.

I have seen all kinds of sales contests in which prizes ranging from stick pins to European trips were offered, and the more of them I have seen, the more thoroughly I have become convinced that the best way to bring in good worthwhile business is to employ hard working dependable salesmen and pay them liberally in real money for their services. Contests have ruined many young salesmen by getting them worked up to the point of making concessions and promises which were not lived up to. There are two ways to win a contest. One is to high-pressure old customers into over-buying, the other to sell those who have not been sold because of doubtful credit. Both methods are poor business.

Often a man will give you a fine picture of his own character by abusing people who do not happen to agree with him or perhaps have refused to do business with him. It's a pretty good idea to keep quiet about anybody unless you can truthfully say something nice about him.

Most any clerk can fit you to a hat, pair of shoes or a suit of clothes, but you must fit yourself for that which you hope to be.

If we would study the failures and profit by their mistakes and then be man enough to face our faults, and correct them, there would be little question as to our success. When I was not bringing in as much business as another salesman I did not belittle his success and look for faults in him. The man whose faults I started looking for were my own and I usually had little trouble finding them. I never became discouraged because some other salesman was better than I. Not at all, for I did not look upon myself as being the best salesman with the organization but the best salesman I knew how to be.

Sales resistance is often a demonstration of the superiority of mind over matter.

He said, "And the greatest of all is Charity." He did not say that you need wait until you found a widow with hungry children, who had been turned into the street before you start giving. Quite likely a few smiles and kindly thoughts given to those who are hungry for them, or giving others the right to live their lives, and run their business as they want to run it, might be all the charity expected of you.

Self assurance, absolute honesty and truthfulness are the best ammunition a salesman can take along, when he goes out hunting for business.

You must either have a boss, or be one.

He had a hundred dollar bill, which he changed into five twenties, and these he put in different pockets, then turning to me he said, "When a salesman is getting around the country he cannot afford to have his money all in one bill. It is better to have several, and then if one is lost, it does not hurt so much." Knowing how he had always concentrated his efforts on selling one big firm in each town, I said, "For the same reason I have always tried to have five customers in a town in the place of one."

He bought the finest stationery he could, employed the best stenographer obtainable, and was very particular about his letters being written "just so." But he used one of those trick signatures in signing them, and all was lost, because no one could make out the signature.

Listening to the memorized solicitations of some salesmen, and the broadcasting of the average soprano singer, has had much to do with the converting of many to the "silence is golden" idea.

A real family, an honest to goodness job, good health and intelligent thrift will make a contented and respected man out of just an ordinary fellow.

I used to work for a sales manager whose pet line was, "Get in the right mental attitude, if you expect to succeed." There is a lot of truth in that statement. I believe it applies to salesmen more than to any other men in business. I have never known a man to make good in selling, whose home life was not what it should be. I wouldn't give a thin dime for the salesman who has a breakfast table battle with his wife every morning. And he is not at his best if he has a wife who is continually nagging him or keeping his nose to the grindstone.

It is better to see the point than get stuck.

Examining a basket of berries he said, "The top layer looks good but those underneath are no good." The grocer answered, "And that can often be said about customers. Their dress would indicate that they are all right, but when we extend them credit, we find out that they are no good whatever." Each knew what he was talking about.

The way to get the best of a man is to do your best by him.

Whatever success you may be enjoying is due to the interest others have taken in you, because of what you are, or what you have done, and are capable of doing.

An employee is the silent partner of a firm, who shares in the profits but not in the losses.

The longer you delay settling a complaint the more convinced the customer becomes that he is right.

A friend of mine once said to me, "I often make long trips in my auto and I always travel at a regular speed which I know to be safe. I do not deviate much from that set speed. Many pass me seemingly in a great hurry to get some where but generally I pass them later in the day. Some times they are in the ditch and sometimes they are by the roadside waiting for the wrecking car to tow them in." Running autos and businesses have much in common. So far as the business is concerned the man with ordinary intelligence who has in addition plenty of energy and the will to stick steadily to the job generally gets farther along the Road to Success than does the fellow whose business life is marked by bursts of speed and flashes of brilliancy. Look around at our greatest business successes and you will find that they are not so awfully smart as much as they are intelligent and persistent workers.

The mind guides the hand, it grasps the pen, the muscles move, and the name is written on the dotted line. And it is the mind of the salesman dominating the mind of the buyer that brings that about.

The jazz life does not make for savings accounts and yet savings accounts or some equally sound investment are all that is between any of us and the poor house when age or misfortune overtake us. A savings account, and an endowment life policy or old age income insurance makes for self respect without which no one can succeed.

The secret of success is hard work. Maybe that is why it has remained a secret to so many.

The public determines what you and your business are worth to the community, and its appraisal is going to be accepted, no matter what you think about it.

When you get a close up view of celebrities they look just like ordinary human beings, but none of us believe it until we see for ourselves.

It matters not what you are employed to do, Loyalty is that "something else" than is expected of you.

A prizefighter may go down, but he is usually up before the count of ten. A drowning man goes down three times before he stays down. But when the average salesman goes down —he's down.

When a man loses interest in the worth while things of life he is just as dead as he will ever be.

Sincerity is one of the first milestones along the road to success.

A sales solicitation that is dotted with lying seldom gets the name on the dotted line.

I was having lunch with a friend, who had made his millions through speculation, and when the waiter handed him the menu, he glanced over it and said, "I can't eat. I have no appetite whatever. Do you know I have not averaged three hours sleep a night for more than two weeks." Then I took the menu and ordered a lunch that would have satisfied the appetite of a farm-hand. And I thought of the eight or ten hours good restful sleep I was enjoying each night. Then I realized I was rich.

In the Game of Life the percentage of wins on bluff is just about the same as in poker.

Success in business comes from the confidence the public has in us, in our business methods, and the thing we are selling. Every failure can easily be traced to the loss of confidence in one or the other.

I have experienced little or no trouble in getting in to see many of the most famous men of our time, and the heads of our largest industries, but believe me, I have had my troubles in getting an audience with the second assistant secretary to the third vice-president of many concerns.

I asked the president of a large bank how many people he had working for him and he answered, "To tell you the truth, I don't know. I suppose we have several hundred on the floors above, but I do not get up there once a month." I could not resist thinking if not saying. "Then you have very few people working for you. They are working for salary checks. Maybe if you were to show an interest in them, then they might become interested in you, and the success of your bank."

A salesman once asked me what I was selling, and when I told him he said, "You can have all that you want, since I understand it is the hardest stuff in the world to sell." I answered that while it was hard to sell, I was mighty glad of it. He said, "I don't get you." And then I explained what I meant. "If it were easy to sell," I said, "then some such fellow as you would be selling it and getting about as much salary, per month, as I get per week, and I would be out of a job." I have never looked for something that was easy to sell because I have had sense enough to know that only that which was hard to sell offered me an opportunity to make a better salesman of myself, a better salary, and a reputation that would be worth something to me. In looking for something that is hard to sell you do not have to wait in line, because mighty few salesmen are looking for that kind of a job. It takes hard work to sell anything hard to sell, but I have never known of anything of worth, that work would not sell. On, the other hand, I have never known a man to get anywhere in life by selling something that was easy to sell. In fact he is not a salesman, but an order taker. It has been by doing what others have failed to accomplish or were afraid to attempt that has brought success to the captains of America's great industries.

The difference between a wise investor and a fool speculator is that one wins while the other loses.

Many young men are held down, by being held up by their parents.

Poetry and music are to tired nerves just what the gentle rain is to the parched flower, or a kind word is to a tired soul.

Promoters frequently offer me an opportunity to "get in on the ground floor" but I decline with thanks for I have noticed that it is always the ground floor doors the sheriff puts padlocks on.

If you want to succeed in selling, be just as particular about investigating the firm you contemplate going with, as they are going to be about investigating you. A salesman is known by the company he represents, and you are going to share their reputation, be it good or bad. A firm whose business methods are not what they should be will offer you far more money than would any good reliable concern, but do not let that influence you. To accept would be to ruin your future in the business world. It is far better you take less money with a firm whose reputation you can enjoy, than to try to live down the sins of an unreliable concern, and share the name that their crooked methods have brought them. Get with a good reliable firm, and stay with them, and keep on staying with them, and you will win out in the long run. When you are well on your way to success with them, you will receive many flattering offers from other firms, but keep staying where you are. Going from one firm to another is the habit of the failure. It will make a bum of any man. After a while no firm will want you, because they know you have the habits of a gypsy, and they do not care to waste their time on you.

It is said that by the time a man has reached the age of fifty, he has made his own face. As a mans face reflects the life he lives, the faces of some make very interesting reading.

Memory only offers happiness to those of tomorrow, who rightly live today.

There is no better brain food than the swallowing of false pride.

It is usually those who have lost their standing in the business world that are swept off their feet by adversity.

Getting distance on the radio is like getting a lot of money—worth very little to you after you get it.

Social climbers are usually the "fall-guys."

I have no secrets of my own, refuse to become the custodian of those of my friends, have never turned a key in the lock on my desk or my correspondence files, and my wife is at perfect liberty to go through my pockets any time she might want to do so, though she never has. My only reason for relating these little truths, is that I have found them splendid worry cures, and some friend might profit by them.

Salesmen should never find fault with prospective buyers for making objections for it is the overcoming of them that makes them think, know their business, and become better salesmen.

Those who never trust to luck are usually lucky.

Never become satisfied with your job, except as an opportunity to make yourself worthy of a better job.

Good golfers are little interested in winning a game from a fellow who anyone could easily beat, and a good salesman never gets much enthusiasm out of selling a man who any salesman could sell.

Success comes from working yourself, not your friends.

Dollars do not buy happiness. Happiness is a thing that friends give us.

When an employee becomes self-satisfied, his employer usually becomes dissatisfied, and then comes the parting of the ways.

To use a friend is to abuse a friend, and likewise lose a friend.

Fifty years ago they were schoolmates. They met again, one a prosperous business man, the other a "down-and-outer." The latter complained that he had never had any luck. The prosperous one answered, "Neither have I."

He said, "Nobody is going to get the best of me." Inasmuch as I happened to know much about the life he was living, and his business methods, the thought struck me, that those looking for "the best" would be using rather poor judgment in coming to him for it.

Some people are still laboring under that old superstitious belief that drinking tea or coffee at night will keep them awake. Suppose they do, they will not cause you to keep the neighbors awake until two o'clock in the morning with the singing of "Sweet Adeline."

"Sharp knives make tender meat" but sharp words harden the hearer's heart and reduce the possibility of future contact and profitable association.

"Nothing succeeds like success." That is, if the successful succeed in holding on to the fruits of their success.

Don't wait until you are broke before you start to mend your ways.

Shut yourself in a dark room and in time you will go stone blind. Close your eyes to the opportunities that are everywhere about you, and look only upon the dark side of life, and you will be so blind that you will never see success.

Real salesmen know that the beaten path is for beaten men.

The fellow who does not need a boss is usually the man who is selected to be one.

"Everything comes to the man who waits"—until he has his plans perfected, so he can go after that which he wants.

A story that has to be told in an undertone is just as well left untold.

The salesman who uses plain common-sense in selling, can usually sense the wants of the customer.

I have never felt the need of big words to express my own thoughts, nor have I ever had a feeling that I was missing much in not knowing the meaning of many of them that I might understand what those who used them were talking about.

There should be a law passed to protect innocent defenseless babies against having their parents inflict upon them names that would be far more suitable for Pullman cars and nickel cigars. An easy to say and easy to remember name is a great asset to a salesman or any other man in business. It is just about as bad to give a child the names of a lot of personal friends or deceased relatives forcing him to use two or three initials that mean nothing. Given names breed friendliness. How many well known men can you call to mind who have not used their given names? Like nearly all men, I had two given names—Ormsby Coleman Cox, if you please. I wrote my name 0. C. Cox. The initials meant nothing to those who wanted to call me by name. My friends coined names, and to them I was Coxey, Coley, OC and CC. In fact I was like a lost dog at a county fair, I would answer to any name. One day I made up my mind that I was going to have a name and I became Coleman Cox. Since then I have never had a nickname. I always use my full name in introducing myself, answering phones, etc. That has caused others to do so. It causes people to feel they know me better and become more friendly, and that is the way I want them to feel toward me and that is the way every salesman should want people to feel about him. Initials are meaningless. Use your given name. While initials may be easier for you to write, you will profit more by making it easy for people to know your name and remember it.

A good salesman will never quote a man a price until he has first made him want that which he is selling, and then the price does not often stand between him and the closing of the sale.

We seldom have much trouble in getting along with people that we really know. Some of these days certain business concerns are going to find this out, and when they do, they will have their credit men calling on their customers, becoming personally acquainted with them, and studying their business, after which there will be fewer harsh letters written, and incidentally fewer customers lost.

Work is a mighty hard thing to keep track of. A man will go to an employer saying he has been looking for work everywhere, but cannot find it. The employer gets busy, finds work and gives it to him. Then the employer expects work from the employee, and when he does not get it, pays him off and starts him out looking for work again and the chances are he never finds it.

8
It Seems To Me

When I see a new automobile going down the street, it reminds me of what I was. And when I see an old dilapidated car on the scrap heap, it reminds me of what I am to be.

It is a big man who can logically think out a problem which vitally affects him and then accept the conclusion, even if it is against his desire or inclination.

When you have nothing to worry about you are not doing much, and not doing much may supply you with plenty of future worries.

Some of these days our colleges will require all students to take a post-graduate course in Human Nature before starting out in the world to earn a living by the application of the knowledge they have gained through years of schooling. I would suggest as instructors, a hotel clerk, a Pullman porter and a street car conductor, for these types are the best judges of human nature.

I have worked for just as many sales managers who were "human fire extinguishers" as "spark plugs."

No man can work successfully without a system, and those who are most successful, willingly accept and use the system that their employers have given years of time to perfecting.

When I was a boy I had the fastest running rabbit dog in Kentucky. In fact he was so fast he would run over the rabbit and lose him. I have met a lot of fast talking salesmen who remind me of that dog. They talked so fast to slow thinking prospects that they lost many sales.

Kind deeds emanate from a heart that is overflowing with love and sympathy for others — and meanness is just the opposite.

So many men get the idea, that to appear dignified they must wear faces without smiles.

Some men give their wives a monthly allowance of so many dollars; some an allowance of time, affection and consideration. Some give them both and live happy lives.

As a protection against thefts and robberies office clocks should be made a part of safes and cash registers. Then a good part of the employees would always be watching them.

You are either going to be a "go-getter" or a "regretter."

No man can afford to "don't care."

Listen to the voice of Experience, and experience fewer failures.

An unoccupied automobile stood by the side of the street with its engine running. Not far away stood a salesman, wondering who he should call on. Both were burning up energy, and getting nowhere.

To most people, a great thinker is one who tells them just what they already think.

While a man may get mad at you for refusing to loan him money, he cannot but respect your good judgment.

Someone was telling me that we have three kinds of liars—plain, statistical, and damned. I expect you have met them all.

I heard a very successful man say, "The only people I like to have call me Mister are servants." I heartily agree with him.

Working and talking at the same time can be done where neither the work nor the talk calls for thinking.

An idle rumor is never idle.

There is a title of an old song that should be painted on the wall of every sales room, "It Makes No Difference What You Were, It's What You Are Today."

I have never met a successful business man who did not like to talk about his business, and I have always given them the opportunity to do so. By asking questions, and being a good listener, I know sooner or later they would talk themselves into doing business with me.

A cat has only nine lives. Most men live many more.

Instead of trying to get even with an enemy you can inflict far more torture by getting ahead of him.

All great successes, and failures, have come from doing "little things."

To many men, selling is unloading something on someone who has no use for it.

Advertising is asking people to do something for you, and the more of their time you consume in the asking, the less chance you have of getting them to do it.

I heard of a man who took a prescription to a drug store, and when the salesman looked at it he said, "I see this is for nervousness. If in the place of taking drugs you would go to the park and enjoy the beautiful flowers and sunshine, you would be all right." In a few minutes he was on his way to the park with a twenty dollar camera the salesman had sold him, which at least was more profitable to the store than the filling of a sixty cent prescription.

Nine times out of ten it is the first few words spoken by the salesman in making his first call that makes the sale—or loses it.

No goal—no gold.

Have you a mental picture of what you are to be in years to come, or are you just drifting along, you know not where?

Be honest and truthful with your banker, your lawyer and your doctor. Also be honest with yourself, and you will make fewer calls on others asking them to help you out of your troubles.

What Luck I have had, I have worked for.

Nearly every failure who is having a hard time getting along can tell you of the days when he was prosperous. And nearly every prosperous man can tell you of the days when he was a failure and had a hard time getting along.

The owner of a large Seattle store was about ready to sign a contract with me that would total fifteen thousand dollars. Hearing our price was to advance in a few days, I called and told him that he could save three thousand dollars by signing his contract at once. His attitude changed entirely as he said, "If I had a man working for this firm who would take advantage of such confidential information to lose us three thousand dollars, I would discharge him immediately." I lost all chance of getting his business and rightly so. It was a lesson to me.

Get this: Life is a one way road. We can't go back and correct the mistakes of yesterday but we can do our best to avoid making them over and over again.

Finding a job is a real job, and when a man confesses he cannot find a job he often confesses he is not worthy of one.

If you are a failure with your present firm you will be the same sort of a failure with another firm —unless you mend your ways.

Hot tempers are usually responsible for heated arguments.

A new sales manager came with our company and the first thing that he did was to call a meeting of all salesmen, and asked each to bring along his prospect files. When the men had piled their files on the table, and were seated, he entered the room. He asked if all prospect records were in, and the salesmen answered that they were. Pulling over a waste basket, he dumped them all into it, and turning to the men said, "Now we are going to start all over again, and get business, in the place of regrets and promises." And they brought in the business, much of it being from firms who had never heard of us before, because the time of our salesmen had been taken up in calling on "promising" prospects.

A factory whistle is just as musical to the young man who is headed for success, as a road-house jazz band is to the one headed for failure.

As we grow more sensible we become less sensitive.

Sympathy is all right, except for personal use.

If salesmen could only become Confident, without being Conceited.

Living the night life keeps many from thinking of the things that they did during the day without thinking.

When business slows down a little the first thing many firms do is quit advertising and reduce their sales force. One of America's most successful business men immediately increases his advertising when people quit buying, and when they again start buying they buy his products, the worth of which have by wise advertising been stenciled upon their minds.

Most failures are those who were foolish enough to take their own advice.

Boy Scouts are taught never to close their eyes on a day until they can call to mind at least one good act they have done. Many men would spend sleepless nights if they were to try to be Good Scouts.

A helpful suggestion is always appreciated by a merchant and evidence of interest in the success of his business will often get a salesman an order, when a cold blooded sales talk would make no impression.

Sales managers and not the motion picture industry gave us our first "Talkies."

Killing time is not murder—it's suicide.

Work is just doing what we feel we have to do. Happiness is doing the same thing because we enjoy it.

I am serving notice on the wide, wide world that if I am ever on a jury that is trying a man for killing the talkative pest that deprived him of the opportunity to read his newspaper on the train or street car while on the way to the office that I will vote for his acquittal and buy him a gold service star.

Many salesmen talk so much they do not give the prospect who said "No" a chance to change his mind.

I have met far more salesmen who were oversold on themselves than they were on that which they were selling.

Money may be filthy lucre but my experience has been that it is those without it who treat us the dirtiest.

Where both have used their heads to get ahead, then two heads are better than one. Take married life as an example.

When an employee cannot get along with his fellow employees probably it is because they are going ahead of him.

Everyone is looking for a doctor who can cure them of their ailments without taking from them their pleasures or the habits that cause the ailments.

We hear much about "sales helps" and here are the ones that I have found most essential during my forty-two years a salesman: A firm that has the confidence of the people; a product that is made right, priced right, and wanted, a sales manager who is long on constructive suggestions and short on conceit; a shipping clerk who sees to it that deliveries are made when wanted, and in good condition; an accountant who writes friendly and diplomatic letters to customers in the place of sarcastic or sassy ones. Any salesman can sell if he has these all important "helps," and no salesman can sell without them.

Many have their worst disappointments when the worst does not happen.

Salesmen not fired with enthusiasm are soon fired.

The Lord has heard more prayers since aviation started than He has heard in years.

When a fellow tells me he is "Working For" a certain firm, then in the same breath starts lambasting their business methods, and everyone associated with the firm from president to the office boy, I know I have met another liar.

In the eyes of the family, father is a sort of the century plant and wilts when the son shines.

To the boy in the primary school, Dad is a very smart man. When he reaches high school, Dad makes the mistake of trying to help him with his lessons and then his reputation begins to slip. And when he is in college, Dad writes what he has to say on "stationery" supplied by his bank and signs his name.

Clothes reflect the individuality and personality of the man—or the individuality and personality of his wife, as the case may be.

There is no greater waste of time than to read without thinking.

My list of "good men I have met" is not made up entirely of those who never took a drink, used tobacco or swore.

Happiness is crowded out of our lives by wanting that to which we are not entitled and worrying over things that never happen.

As a salesman I have never been able to enjoy a ball game or matinee during business hours because of the still small voice that was continually saying to me, "There is someone somewhere who is waiting to buy that which you are being paid to sell."

The surest way of not making good is to be afraid you won't.

Have you ever talked to yourself somewhat along these lines, "You poor 'Simp.' Don't you know that you are not kidding anybody but yourself? That the Boss is wise to you trying to make the grade in low, and unless you go into high pretty soon you are going to be without a job? Increase in salary? Why, you are not making yourself worth what you are getting. From right now on, you are going to work, and you are going to work as you never did before, until you make a man of yourself." A talk of that kind is often very helpful.

Our thoughts are but mental pictures, and it is well that we alone see some of them.

A right good time to overcome sales objections is when you are making that which you expect to sell.

Those who fear the worst is yet to come can little enjoy the best that has already come.

The average fellow who prides himself on being an optimist is as artificial as Hollywood love, and is trying to hide the fact that he is broke, all in, down and out.

Doctors usually advise salesmen to eat spinach, knowing they need grit.

When an automobile manufacturer brings out a new model he does not waste his time looking over old cars he has made in the past, but gives his time and thoughts to making a still better car. I am sure if salesmen would quit talking about what they have done in the past, and give their time and thought to getting more business today they would get along much better.

I can remember when it was only the farmer who watered his stock.

Opportunities are jobs that were made into positions by men of brains and energy, which brought them fame and fortune.

To the industrious we must credit the industries.

I have sold thousands of men that I never expected to sell, and have failed to sell many more that I felt absolutely sure of selling.

Any employee can make himself worth more, worth less, or worthless.

Life is just what we make it. That's why some are happy.

I am opposed to capital punishment, whether it be the breaking of a fellow's neck, or breaking him in a business way.

There is not a human being living who could not be a success in life if he were but satisfied to be that which nature prepared him to be, and would work to be it. Ninety per cent of the failures are men who have been trying to do that which they wanted to do, and for which they were not at all fitted. Be yourself, and be successful.

However good they may be, others' ideas are worthless unless you build them into your character.

Merchandise, like men, has character, and it is poor business to have anything to do with either unless the matter of character is established beyond question.

Your understanding of others, and their understanding of you, will have much to do with your becoming an outstanding man.

After making considerable investigation Forbes tells us that the average successful American business man is fifty-five and a half years old, weighs a hundred and eighty-one pounds, stands five feet ten and one-half inches, wears a sixteen collar, a seven and a quarter hat, and an eight and a half shoe. How do you measure up?

All of the "floor-walkers" are not found in department stores. Some forty years ago I heard Ike Hoffman, who lived in my home town down in Kentucky say, "I was head over heels in debt and for weeks I had walked the floor every night without a wink of sleep. One morning about two o'clock the thought struck me that the wrong fellow was doing the floor-walking; that it was those I owed should be doing it, and so I got in bed, went to sleep, and have been sleeping good ever since." That's another way of looking at it.

These are days when owners of cemeteries are about the only people who can truthfully advertise, "Once a customer, always a customer."

I suppose there is a lot to psychology and yet I know a man who is a wonderful salesman and he doesn't know there is such a science.

What this world needs is more young men in overalls learning trades, and making themselves independent. The manager of any savings bank will tell you that he sees far more fingernails with grease under them than those showing a beautiful polish.

Only satisfied salesmen can make satisfied customers.

Winners of bridge, golf and other games are those whose thoughts were concentrated upon winning games and not prizes. Salesmen whose minds are on making sales succeed while those thinking only of increased salaries fail to earn what they are already receiving.

Some buy bouquets of florists while others keep on begging you and me for them by asking for our honest opinion of them and their business.

There may be some truth in the old adage, "there is nothing in a name" but I am going to keep right on buying all stuff that is in tiny cans by the name on the outside.

Merchants open their doors to display their merchandise; but many people open their mouths only to display their ignorance.

I have no sympathy whatever for myself. I am getting all that is coming to me.

I have frequently asked buyers, "Now that you have given me this order, may I ask you which of the many reasons I gave you for doing so, most impressed you?" Many have answered, "I was interested in your business by a friend, who has been doing business with your company for many years. While I was attentive to your talk, and was glad to have you answer some questions I had in mind, I cannot think of any particular thing you said that was responsible for your order." Maybe he couldn't but I could. And that particular thing was, that a satisfied customer made the sale—not me.

There are many things to be accomplished by lying, the first of which I would list, the loss of self respect; then the confidence and respect of others.

Autoists see so many "Speed limit 20 miles an hour" signs they pay little attention to them, but a little town in Texas had its signs read, "20 miles an hour or $19.90." They read that one.

I am still placing my bets on the success of the young man who spends his money for overalls in place of permanent waves.

What I cannot understand about some people is the little that they understand.

"I am not at all interested in what you are selling, but I do want a good salesman, and if you want to make more money than you are getting, I will be glad to talk to you." Every salesman has heard that time and again, and many have made the mistake of leaving a business in which they were successful, to become failures. My answer has always been, "Just how can you look upon me as being a good salesman, when I am unable to intelligently explain my business to you, and show you how you could profitably use that which I am selling?"

Those who know most, know that which isn't worth knowing.

Men do not always like to be told they are that which they rather pride themselves on being. I was told to call on the owner, of a very big business, who was said to glory in the reputation he had of being the meanest man any salesman ever approached. When I entered his office, he looked up from his desk and growled. "Well, 'wotcha want." I answered, "Nothing at all, except that I wanted to see you. I have long wanted to see the man who prides himself on being the meanest man living. A man who thinks he can build a successful business by making enemies." He stared at me a moment, and then a smile covered his face as he said, "Who has been telling you that stuff?" No man was ever more courteous than that fellow was to me, and when I left him, I had a mighty nice order.

Have you ever noticed that it is usually the "moral bankrupts" who become financial bankrupts?

When a salesman I have never known before comes dashing into my office with hand extended, I feel more like saying good-bye, than howdy.

It was long years before "your credit is good" became a business slogan that men signed the Declaration of Independence.

Have your likes and dislikes. Advertise your likes, and let your dislikes be your most guarded secrets.

I never was a "letter writing salesman" because I always figure that if I could not interest a prospect in my business by talking to him face to face, I could not sell him by writing him letters. Then I never wanted our firm to find out that letter writing would bring in the business, because I knew that they could employ better letter writers than I am at less cost than my salary. I am a strong believer in "Tell'm n' Sell'm."

Only those who are prepared for the worst enjoy the best.

The greatest time saving move ever made by bankers was the leaving of their private offices to work out in the open, where a dozen or more can hear them say "NO" as well as one.

So often we hear fathers say, "I do not want my son to go without the things I wanted and had to work so hard for when I was a boy." Maybe it was wanting and working that made them successful, and their success is responsible for the failure of their sons.

Thinking how to do a thing cuts out about 80 per cent of the work of doing it.

The difference between a banker and a personal friend is, that the banker loans on what he Knows a man to be worth, and a personal friend loans on what he Thinks him to be worth. One of them usually loses money.

Cutting the price on merchandise that sells itself at its regular price is a confession on the part of the dealer that he is not as good a salesman as a cake of soap, package of cigarettes, pound of cheese, can of coffee or whatever it might be.

Saving saves slaving.

Before excusing your failure on the ground that you were born of poor parents, try and call to mind some outstanding successful man who was born of rich parents.

Soon after I came with our company, nineteen years ago, I studied my solicitations to find out the points I had been making that had produced business, and these I built into one solicitation, which I am still using. These thoughts are old to me, but they are just as new and convincing to prospects of today as they were to those of years ago. Only salesmen who like to hear themsleves talk feel the need of a new solicitation for every prospect.

We profit more by listening to the Experience of failures than we do by listening to their Advice.

Since you never heard a grouch referred to as having a wonderful personality, is it not true that this so-called personality is nothing more than the outward showing of the inner man?

Our most fluent talkers take as their subject, "Now here is what I would do," while those who know more say less, but it's worth more.

There is such a thing as a "confidential concession." Our sales manager once made a voluntary concession to an old customer. Within a week they had whispered their experience around to other customers of ours, and they all started asking for like concessions, which we denied them, and they quit doing business with us, as did the other firm at the expiration of its contract. We were years in recovering from the "confidential concession."

If you will glance at the automobile advertising in the newspapers, and the suits filed for the alienation of a husband's affections, you will note there is considerable difference in the imaginary worth of second-hand cars and second-hand husbands.

The rungs on the ladder of success are made of big ideas.

Buyers are strong for brevity. It has taken me weeks to get one of them to quit saying "No" and speak a word having just one more letter in it.

Before you condemn an advertising medium for not bringing customers to your door, as it does for your competitor, it might be well for you to give a little thought to your competitor's business methods, and the improving of your own, that your advertising may be as believable and profitable as his.

Self-confidence is the child of Fearlessness and lives on truth, honesty and clean morals.

We have two kinds of Satisfied people. Those who are satisfied with themselves, and those we are satisfied with. One of the two make very satisfied companions and friends.

When a man marries for money it's a case of "a fool and his money are soon parted."

Fools shooting off their mouths start men shooting guns, and so we keep on having wars.

This so called "sales resistance" we hear so much about is nothing more than the mental condition of a prospective buyer who has backbone enough to keep on saying "No" to a weak-kneed salesman who cannot interestingly, intelligently, enthusiastically and convincingly talk his business.

The only people I long to get "even with" are those who have been so wonderfully kind to me.

Wives suspect most of their husbands, expect the least from them.

No man can be honest without being truthful.

No employer will stand for an employee laying down on the job.

Mr. Thomas A. Edison once told me he first found out what the people wanted, and if he thought it could be produced at a price they could afford to pay, plus a reasonable profit to the manufacturer and dealer, he went to work on it. Many producers think that all they have to do is to make a thing, employ the services of a "wildcat" advertising agency, and a high-pressure sales manager to unload it on the public.

It is hard to make a woman believe anything and everything—unless it's about her husband.

The street car was crowded, and I heard one woman say to another, "The school teachers of today are impossible. My boy is not learning a thing." A boy of about ten years was seated beside her, and when he arose to give his seat to an old lady who was standing, the mother jerked him back in the seat and told him to stay there. Poor school teachers. The odds are certainly against them teaching some children anything.

The less a salesman knows about his business the longer it takes him to tell it, and the less liable he is to make a sale.

The owners of radios are not so much interested in television that they may see those putting on the programs, but they are living in hopes that announcers who try to be funny, and love to hear themselves talk will be able to see the expressions on their faces as they jump from their chairs, dash to the radio and turn their dials to other stations.

It is the decreasing of a list of prospects by making them customers that increases a salesman's chances of holding his job.

Nature puts your eyes in the front of your head that you might look ahead, and go ahead.

Firms whose output is increasing their income are not worried about the outlook.

Some employees enjoy a good reputation until they quit their jobs, and then they find out that it was not their reputation, but that of the firm they were associated with, that they had been enjoying.

When I hear a man speaking of MY business, MY home, MY car, MY this and that, I know I have met a most Selfish individual.

Another good way of making friends is to start every argument with the thought of losing it.

He was a Gypsy Salesman. That is to say, he was always going from one job to another. I met him recently and asked him what he was doing. He winked, and whispered, "I am selling insurance." I knew he was not selling insurance because no man can sell anything of which he is ashamed.

If you will divide what you think by two, and deduct it from ten per cent of what the neighbors think of you, you will have a pretty good idea as to your actual worth.

It takes a collector to find people out—nearly always out.

We form our opinion of people from what we hear and read, and of manufacturers, by what we find in tin cans and cartons.

I have never seen an architect around a building showing a hod-carrier how to carry a hod, a brick-layer how to lay brick, or a carpenter how to saw a board, but I have seen executives of large concerns trying to tell factory foremen what to do and how to do it; sales managers how to sell; advertising managers what to write and what medium to use, shipping clerks how to pack and ship, and the accountant how to get in the money.

Men do not fail because of changed business conditions, but because they were not big enough men to meet changed conditions.

Some people have an idea that they owe themselves a good time, and that is why they don't pay anyone else.

Business never was so sick that hard work wouldn't cure it.

No salesman wants to live a dog's life but the bulldog has some ideas about holding on until he wins his fight.

Create an interest in what you are selling, build that interest into enthusiasm and then write out your order.

An honest salesman is a man who blames himself, and not the prospect, for not having made a sale.

The one best way to systematize a business is to humanize it. Business is, after all, "just men" working to a common purpose. It is but human nature for us to want to help those who help us to succeed either in running a business, or holding down a job.

A man looks better and feels better when his tailor has pressed his suit than he does when a lawyer does it.

A man may be the worst kind of a failure, and still become an outstanding success, by changing his way of Thinking.

In the mind of youth, wealth, power and high place brings happiness. The man of fifty who has learned the true lesson of life knows that happiness which comes from either or all depends on how either or all have been won.

The fellow I think is funny is so much funnier to me than the fellow who thinks he is funny.

You have seen a few men working on buildings, and dozens loafing around watching them. In fact, I suspect you have seen the same thing inside many buildings.

The reason many employees do not grow old is because the Boss carries all the responsibilities.

Another reason some salesmen do not sell more is because they only show and talk articles that especially appeal to them, which often interest buyers less than many other things that go to make up their lines.

A man who is a "bull peddler" is easily "cowed."

When a man starts giving advice he is usually too old to set a bad example.

A smile is the one greeting that all people of the world understand.

Remembering past failures leaves little room in our minds for thoughts upon which to build our future success.

Your employer thought there was something in you, and your pay envelope contains his estimate of what has come out.

When a young man is thrown on his own resources he either makes a success in life or no longer keeps us in doubt as to his being a failure.

A combination of industry, intelligence and thrift is the shortest way from the mediocre to the worthwhile positions in life.

Success is wrapped in responsibility.

Thirty minutes is about the listening limit for an after dinner talk and every added minute lessens the value of all that has been said previously.

It is said, "Everything happens for the best," but are you one of the best?

Making a sale is one thing, and making a customer is another thing. Both should be made at the same time.

The only way to get ahead is by getting something into the head you have.

Ideas are a salesman's only tools with which to work.

We are what others make us, and they usually make us what we show ourselves worthy of being.

There are far more men who have a million dollars than there are those who are worth a million dollars.

When a woman speaks of her "late husband" you don't know whether he is dead, or a "golf hound."

"Credit to those to whom credit is due" is not only an old maxim, but a mighty good business policy.

While driving in the country one day my wife saw a weed by the roadside that had a rather attractive blossom, and she brought it home, planted it in the garden, watered, cultivated it and loved it. In time it was the most beautiful plant in the garden. Often when I am watering it, the thought comes to me, that along the road of life there are many human beings that are looked upon as being just as worthless as a weed, and that they, too, might grow into real worth-while citizens if they were taken up, cultivated and given a little love just as my wife has given this weed from the roadside.

Unfortunately, those who pride themselves on saying just what they think, usually have nothing but unkind thoughts.

Many are going to dislike you because they know none of your faults, and feel confident that you know many of theirs.

Judges have the power to lock jurors in a room and keep them there until they arrive at some decision. Every salesman has often wished he could do the same thing with some buyers.

You don't have to make a better mouse trap to have the world make a path to your door. All you have to do is circulate the report you have some money that is not working.

It does not always follow that the person you are looking upon as being your best friend considers you his or her friend, and therefore the secrets you trust them with are repeated to their best friends, who pass them along to their best friends until they become public property.

The average salesman is one of two kinds of talkers. He either talks too much, or he doesn't say anything.

The happiness of success comes in achievement.

Crops don't grow unless seed is planted and tended. We acquire friends and business customers by the same method.

Those who are poorly paid usually do poor work and have a good chance of remaining poor.

It is creation of interest that creates a sale.

Those in too great a hurry to get to the front are usually found by the roadside.

The best way to "work" your personal friends is to give them some of your business.

9
As I See It

We are looking forward to the coming of the man who can correct the business and moral wrongs of the world. All that each and every one of us asks of him is, that he find no fault with the way we are running our business or living our lives.

To bring in an order does not necessarily mean that a sale has been made.

Middle age might be described as being somewhere between a night club and a golf club.

Before investing in a "going concern" be sure you find out which way it is going.

Revenge pays big dividends, but only in the form of regrets and unpleasant thoughts.

Wall Street men often go broke because they do not know their stocks. The same thing is true of merchants on Main Street.

The hurry of some executives in consigning advertising matter to the waste basket frequently results in their janitors carrying out more good ideas than they do.

The political party in power will "blushingly" accept all responsibility for any happiness or prosperity that we may enjoy, and unhesitatingly charge every adversity or calamity as "An act of God."

We are told that most of the stars shine with reflected light, and lots of people get by in the same way. Take married men for example.

The employee who is looking for success in finding something soft has but to remove his hat.

Loose living does not make for hard muscles or an agile brain. Athletes must keep physically fit or fall. Brain workers don't offer any exception to the rule.

We object to being "worked" for the money that we have worked for.

Every employer is glad to see an employee look upon himself as being his own boss, provided he takes orders and does not try to give them.

Diplomacy may be all right, but somehow or other I have never been able to draw a line between it and Deceit.

I know a fellow who became overly enthusiastic about a business he was forming, and unloaded a lot of stock on many of his personal friends. The thing blew up, and now he is even without sympathetic friends. Personal friendships are too valuable to try to profit by—in a business way.

Some say there is no harmony in jazz music. Well, I don't know so much about that, but I will say that I have seen little harmony in sales organizations that were overdosed with jazz sales methods.

About the best place to see a gathering of those who talk the loudest about the high cost of living, is in front of a moving picture theatre, fighting their way to the ticket window to pay fifty cents or a dollar to see a picture show that used to cost ten cents. And have you ever heard any one of them complain about picture shows costing too much? Neither have I.

I had rather talk to a man who is hard of hearing than to one who is hard-headed and hard-boiled.

What a difference there is in the friendliness of the salesman who sells things on the "easy-to-pay-plan" and the collector who comes along later.

When an inmate of a prison is released to go out in the world and earn a living, he finds it difficult to get used to the clothes worn by business men. I wonder if college students who have spent several years in corduroy pants, a sweater and no hat, do not have the same feeling.

There is no doubt that the only way a man can improve himself is by thinking. Perhaps the reason for so many failures is that many men look upon "thinking" as a waste of time because their employers ever give them an opportunity to express a thought.

I am frequently asked what my hobby is. Well, during my many years in selling, I have had about every hobby any man could have. If my prospect was a golfer, then golf was my hobby, though I have never played a game in my life. I have never driven a car, but if a prospect wanted to talk about automobiles, we would talk automobiles. I have not fired a gun nor wet a fish line in many years, but if hunting and fishing was the hobby of the man I was calling on, he would soon find out that I was interested in the subject. So while I have never had any particular hobby of my own, I have made right good use of those of others I have done business with. Showing an interest in the thing my prospects were interested in frequently resulted in them becoming interested in the thing I was interested in and selling. As I understand it, a hobby is the doing of something that we like to do, and are happiest in doing. If that be true, then my hobby is my work.

Happiness comes from mental contentment.

We see little change in those we have been closely associated with for many years, but were we separated from them for a while, the difference would be quite noticeable. That is true of the house that you live in. The paint has grown dim with age, but you have not noticed it, because of the change being so gradual. But others notice its dilapidated condition, and to them it is all but an indication of prosperity.

The Strong Man in a circus gets paid for carrying five or six people, while Merchants "carry" hundreds, and are often never paid.

Find no fault with fools, for were it not for others being able to take advantage of the fool things they do, we would have few wise and successful men.

Knowing others is interesting, but success comes from knowing ourselves, our qualifications and limitations.

I had finished reading the evening paper, thrown it aside, and in deep thought was looking down at my feet, when my wife asked, "Are your feet bothering you again?" I answered, "No, I was just wondering how in the world they ever brought me back from where they have taken me."

As I see it, there is a lot of good in all things, however bad they may be. Selfishness is unquestionably the foundation upon which most all wrongs of the world are built, yet I find that it gives me the most worthwhile things of life. I do my best to make others happy, because it makes me happier to see them happy. I cannot give myself a smile, but by wearing one, nearly everyone I meet will give me one. I concentrate my efforts on making those who do business with me successful, because I know it is to others I must look for my success. So, even selfishness is not bad, when rightly used.

After having employed all those needed, it might be well to remove the "Help Wanted" sign from the window, and hang it in front of those employed, so they may know that their help is wanted in running the business. Besides that, it might be well to let them know that the sign is ready to go back in the window.

I so often wonder how doctors make a living by telling people what will cure their ailments, for I have but to mention the fact that I am not feeling exactly well, and everyone wants to give me a sure cure.

There is no man so blind as he who closes his eyes on truth.

There are times when it is almost necessary for the Boss to be a crank, to start some employees going.

"So you are a salesman, are you?" asked the employer of the applicant for a position. "Am I a salesman? Why, I am the best salesman in the world." The employer said, "Well, you are just the fellow I am looking for," and employed him. Weeks passed, and only expense accounts were received from him, and finally he was asked to come in. As he entered the manager's office, he was greeted with, "And so you are the best salesman in the world —Eh?" The fellow shook his head and said, "No. I am only the next best salesman in the world. The best salesman in the world is the fellow who sold you the stuff that you have had me out trying to sell."

So "doggone" many people who come my way seem to have an idea that a friend is a combined money lender, employment agent, one who delights in listening to other people's troubles, and a fellow who should unhesitatingly buy everything offered him, whether he has any use for it or not.

The fellow who keeps his feet on the ground will some of these days have a manager's desk to put them under.

Not knowing when he will ever have a chance of getting another one, a drinking man seldom refuses a drink, and for the same reason women often become engaged to marry worthless no-account men.

There used to be an old fellow down in Kentucky, whose favorite expression was, "He's too sot in his ways." Many sales managers have wasted a lot of time and money in trying to make salesmen out of just such fellows.

Advice would perhaps be much more acceptable if it was not offered in the form of criticism.

Smith told his imaginary troubles to Brown, who enlarged on them considerably, and repeated them to his friend Wilson, who gave them another stretching, and passed them on to Smith's banker, who immediately called Smith's loans. Then Smith had some real troubles. When in difficulty it is a good idea to keep your mouth closed if you want to keep your place of business open.

Salesmen who are thinking only of the profits that they and their firms are to get, make few sales. The way to sell, is to show the buyer where he is going to profit. The profits of the salesman and his firm naturally follow.

Maybe increased cooperation among salesmen has been brought about by so-called "Friendly Rivalry," but I have not seen it. There is no better record to give a salesman to beat than his own record of last year. And there is no better inducement that can be offered him for beating it than an increase in pay.

When a young married man brings home the bacon, and his wife cooks it, after which they eat it, and then she washes the dishes, while he wipes them, a life of happiness is being started, and their names will never be called in a divorce court. And how well I know that to be true, for as Uncle Billy Wise used to say, "I'm done tried it."

Many young men who are hard up, have blown up, and given up, are down because they tried to fly too high.

Give everyone the benefit of a doubt hoping they may be as charitable with you sometime.

The theme song of the liar is, "Now this is the truth."

No two salesmen are worth the same money to any firm. Every salesman should make his own salary.

If you run an obsolete automobile, don't find fault because of others going ahead of you. And follow the same advice in case you are trying to run your business with methods that have long been obsolete.

Young men starting life without any fixed place in mind as to where they are to go, or what they are to do, are often furnished that information by a judge and warden.

A fortune awaits the manufacturer who can turn out a lady's shoe that is large inside and small outside.

I go to church now and then, and frequently the thought comes to me, that a lot of the things the Lord is asked to do for us are things we ought to be doing for ourselves. Too many of us fail to make any effort to answer our own prayers.

Convincing salesmen are in demand, but not the kind who start each day by convincing themselves no one wants to buy that which they are selling.

In employing men I have always placed as much value on what their neighbors thought of them as their former employers.

There is no better cure for disliking people than to do them an act of kindness, for we always like those we have in some way befriended. The nicest thing about the remedy is, that we improve our own disposition so much that fewer people will dislike us.

That they might enjoy the personal satisfaction of getting an order from a firm that has long been listed as "impossible" in place of using their time in selling a number of other firms whose business is just as desirable, and perhaps more profitable, has cost many salesmen their jobs.

A business depression offers many firms an opportunity to rid their payrolls of a number of worthless employees, and puts a lot of fellows out of business who never had any good reason for classing themselves as business men. Maybe it is just as well that we have a depression now and then.

Another dream that does not always come true is the happiness we are going to enjoy when we accumulate a lot of money.

No one will ever have cause to complain about your fault finding if you will keep secret the result of your findings.

"Very quiet. Little building going on." That is the usual answer you get when you ask a plumber about business conditions. In truth, any home that was built a few years ago is a prospect for modern plumbing today. Builders must buy plumbing, while it must be sold to those having homes. Supplying a demand is perhaps easier, but selling offers the plumber a larger and more profitable field.

There are two ways of "taking life easy." One is by imposing upon friends; the other is accomplished by jumping from a ship in mid-ocean. One of the two is highly recommended by friends.

Writers are not supposed to have money—unless they be writers of checks.

A green light means you can go ahead. A greenback often means the same thing.

A cat was stretched out before the fire, and turning to my friend I said, "Lucky cat." He answered, "I'll say he is. He had his eyes open nine days after birth, and here I keep on endorsing notes for fellows, buying worthless stocks, and have been married three times. I often wonder when I will get mine open."

Big business is of course desirable, because it is more profitable. However it is not well to concentrate all sales efforts on the big concerns and pass up the little fellows, for some of these days many of them will be big buyers and their accounts will stay with those who sold them, cultivated them, and helped them grow.

Maybe the reason we Americans do not know how to run this country is that the advice offered us by soap box orators is spoken in a language we cannot understand.

It has been my observation that those who do not believe in God do not believe in anyone nor anything worth mentioning, and few believe in them.

When an employee becomes satisfied with the position he has and the salary he is receiving, he has ceased to grow, and is neither entitled to the job he has nor the pay he gets.

Jealousy is nothing more than a confessed weakness.

Every wife should be interested in her husband's business—and grant him the privilege of running it.

I am opposed to the hanging of men for murder, and I am going to be against hanging entirely when they quit broadcasting "boop-oop-a-doop" songs, and orchestra leaders put a stop to giving us their ideas of how the music to "Home, Sweet Home" and other loved songs should have been written.

Being insistent is all right if one is careful to avoid being insistent about things that are inconsistent, inconsequential, ill-advised, unimportant or untrue.

When remembrance and regrets are lasting, our mistakes have proved profitable.

Unused knowledge yields about the same return as unused tools or idle capital.

A business is much the same as an automobile. It will not run itself, except downhill.

I know a purchasing agent, who after having listened to the talk of salesmen all day, and the ravings of a talkative wife for an hour or more after having reached home, gets mad, puts on his hat and heads for the theatre that is advertising the best "talkie" in town.

I am a strong believer in the law of compensation. When I hear of someone having "good luck" I look upon it as just a payment for the good they have done someone at some time or other. And the same rule applies to those having "bad luck."

The successful man shows what he can do himself, while the failure talks about what he would do if he were someone else.

No best-selling product owes its success to the fact that it is the cheapest to be had, nor have those who have been in business the longest the reputation of selling the cheapest.

It is amusing to hear a parrot repeat what it has heard, which is more than I can say for many people, because that which they repeat is more often dirty scandal than something built of clean uplifting thoughts or humor.

Those who profess to "don't care" are sooner or later overburdened with cares.

Suffering is often the making of character. Most invalids are really very enjoyable company.

To many it is not so much what they do that counts, as who they do, and how much they do them for.

Someone has said that "Fish and company smell after the third day," and I don't know but what he could have gone further and said that our admiration for the personal friends we put on our payrolls lasts hardly that long.

To insure its own success, a firm has but to look after the success of its employees and customers.

The quitting of booze fighting associates is the first step in quitting booze, and that is the hard thing for some men to do.

Employees who credit themselves with knowing more than their employers are usually right. Had their employers known as much about them as they do about themselves, they would never have made the mistake of employing them.

The successful men I have met were neither optimists nor pessimists, but men of just plain common sense.

Worry is brought about by two things. We are afraid we won't get it, and after we do, we are afraid that somebody else will get it.

It is easy for us to trace the success of others to their having taken our advice, and equally easy for us to account for our failures because of our not profiting by the advice of others.

A number of travelers were congregated in the smoking compartment of a Pullman car, talking first about one thing, then another, when one of these loud mouthed fellows, who had been taking the center of the stage as each subject was suggested, proceeded to air his views on the prison situation. It was his contention that the world would be better off if the inmates of all prisons were lined up against a stone wall and shot. A quiet, dignified old gentleman who had been listening, but saying nothing, remarked, "After having lived eighty years, I am convinced there is scarcely a man living, who has not at some time in life been guilty of enough to send him to prison." All became as quiet as death in the car, and it was plain to be seen, that each man was thinking. The first to quietly depart was the original speaker. Soon others got up and left — and I went with them, leaving the old gentleman alone, to perhaps enjoy the satisfaction of having made us all think, perhaps a little more kindly of others.

Showing up late for work invariably makes a liar of a man, and that destroys self respect, as well as the respect of his associates. What is left is not worth mentioning.

While we do not like to listen to the troubles of others, our hearing them frequently causes us to take our own less seriously.

Yes, opportunity knocks. It knocks every knocker out of every opportunity he may have had for opportunity.

Some men never find themselves, and others wish to goodness that they hadn't.

It goes without saying that a salesman should know all there is to know about the thing he is selling, and it is just about as important that he know the man he is to sell. Years ago I remarked to a friend that I was going down to see the manager of a large sales organization about a position, and asked him if he knew the man. He said, "I have never met him, but I see him quite often around the club. He is what you would call a 'nut' at playing solitaire. He will stay up half the night until he beats it." The following morning I made my call, and after considerable talk, my prospects of getting the position looked none too bright. Turning to me he said, "I am afraid that you have not the determination you should have to make a success in this business." Quick as a flash I replied, "Determination! Why man, I was up until two o'clock this morning trying to beat a new game of solitaire a fellow showed me, and I would be at it yet, if I had not beat it." I got the job.

About the only satisfaction that a father gets in advising a son is, that in years to come the son will likely be a father himself.

It so often happens that when a manufacturer cuts a price it means that the merchandise is no good. And when a salesman cuts a price, it means he is no good.

I can remember when the farmer was the happiest of men. In those days he spent his time on his farm, just as the business man puts in long hours in looking after his business. Once a week the farmer would go to the nearest village or town for needed supplies, and his mail, the most important of which was his weekly county paper, which told him what was going on in his locality, and about those he knew, and was interested in. Then came rural route delivery, bringing him the big daily city paper filled with the murders, robberies, business failures, war predictions, and troubles of the world in general, sandwiched in between which there were enough stories of prosperity to induce his sons and daughters to leave home for the "riches and fame" that await them in some big city. Then came the radio, which politicians have so effectively used in convincing the farmer that he is in a deplorable condition, and what he needs is relief, which is his, for the vote. The farmer knows more today than he ever knew, but like most of us he does not profit by what he knows.

Our future pessimists and optimists will be made up of those of today, who, blinded by fear, sold out to men of vision.

Those who know much without knowing it, make most interesting company.

It is not uncommon for people to confess murder or theft, but have you ever tried to get a man or woman to confess that they were living beyond their means?

Those realizing how much they owe themselves, appreciate the fact that they cannot afford to owe others.

The executive of a large concern and I had left his office and were waiting for an elevator to take us to the ground floor, when a small boy, who was a messenger for a telegraph company, hurried down the hall to the elevator, pressed the button a time or two, and with a look of disgust said, "What's the matter with these elevators. I've got no time to be waiting around here like this." My friend looked at me, smiled, and turning to the boy said, "Here is my card. When you can find time to do so, I want you to come in to see me." When he called, he was employed as an office boy. Soon he had a better job, and he has continued to advance, until he has but another move to make, when he will be holding an executive position. Every large concern is looking for the young man who places a value upon time.

About all loud talk does is to keep the prospective buyer from going to sleep.

It matters not how good that which you are selling may be, you will have many objections to overcome. The man making the most sales anticipates these objections, and is prepared to overcome them as fast as they are made.

There are no two better reasons for opening a savings account and buying life insurance, than to see some who are living the last years of their lives in comfort, and others in poverty.

They can't put you in jail for taking a chance. They can only send you to the poor-house.

It is too bad that our point of view is frequently based upon short sightedness.

Our ideals are measurements we expect others to come up to, though we've never done it ourselves.

A clerk is showing the first symptoms of becoming a salesman when he suggests to the prospective buyer an article he knows to be better than the one asked for.

Confidence, enthusiasm, ambition and success are produced by belief, faith and courage.

Friends are the greatest riches in all the world. I think that the forming of Service Clubs was the greatest movement ever started, because they have brought representative men of every known business and profession together, that they might get acquainted and become friends. Yes, they have done more than that. They have grown until they cover the world, and that must and will build up a better friendship between nations.

I can forgive some murderers and thieves, because they might have been to some extent excusable, but the man I cannot forgive, is one who tells me a filthy story. There is no excuse for vulgarity.

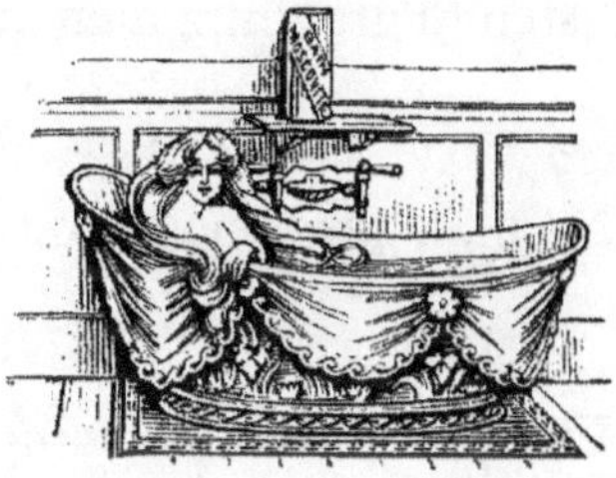

The same fellow who gets mad at the alarm clock that wakes him up in the morning, gets mad when some interested friend tries to get him to wake up to his opportunities.

A determination to make good is a first mortgage on Success.

It always looks easy to sell, when someone else is selling it.

Another waste of time is the making of rules for other people's morals.

Be yourself. To be unnatural is to be uncomfortable and unhappy. To me there is no more pathetic sight than to see some fellow who has by chance come into a vast amount of money, all dolled up in dinner dress, surrounded by a lot of broken down aristocrats, trying to figure out which fork to use in the eating of an unknown dish that has been placed before him, knowing that as soon as that ordeal is over, he is to spend an evening at grand opera. Thank the Lord my financial condition is such that I can still enjoy my corned beef and cabbage, surrounded by real friends, who enjoy real food.

The most convincing proof that a new man can offer that he is not a salesman is bringing in orders from only his personal friends.

We can grab a club and drive away a growling dog, but we are forced to listen to growling men and women.

No man has done his best.

Every employee showing up for work in the morning tells his associates by his facial expression, actions and manner of speech, how things were when he left home.

Remembering the Golden Rule, in all transactions, will come nearer getting you where you want to go from here than will all dogmas and creeds.

Maybe the reason it is so easy for us to see the mistakes of others is, that they were ideas we once had but were afraid to carry out.

More sales are lost because of salesmen thinking the price is too high than because the prospective buyers think so.

You can use a machine in your business, but you cannot make a machine of it.

The fuss that is kicked up every now and then about married women doing the work that men should be doing is never started by their husbands.

The hardest of all men to sell, is the affable man, who greets you with a smile, and unhesitatingly agrees with you in all you say, often anticipating that which you are about to tell him, and wrecking your solicitation by telling it to you. Give me the hard-boiled battler in preference to the agreeable man, and I will answer for more sales.

I know the head of a large concern whose first question asked of a salesman applying for a position is, "Have you any money?" He says that the salesman who is broke and in debt is less than fifty per cent efficient because of worries about his personal affairs.

It so often happens that the most complimentary things said about us are said by those who do not know us.

The theatre is frequently the home of the coward. I mean those who are afraid to be alone with their thoughts.

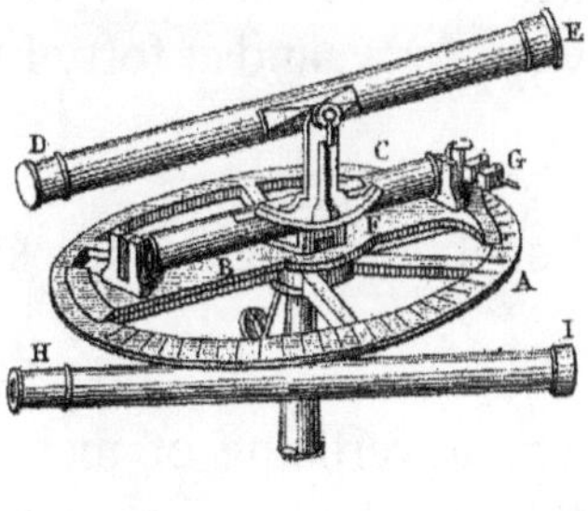

Cultivating hard work until you have formed a love for it, is the way you are going to become successful —if you ever do.

The salesman who boasts, "I never take anything from a grouchy buyer" includes orders with the other things he doesn't take.

Before you boast of having fixed habits, think them over, and perhaps you will find that many of them need fixing.

Success is nothing more than the expression of Character.

A young man has sprung another "How old is Ann" on me. He writes he is just starting in selling, and would like to have me tell him how to approach a prospect. I suppose I have approached some fifty thousand or more, and if I have ever approached any two of them alike, I don't know it.

When a product excells it sells and sells.

Those who are waiting for "lucky breaks" are usually broke.

If fellows would only be as nice to us after having induced us to do them favors as they were during the inducing procedure!

I asked a gentleman of ninety how he managed to reach such a ripe old age. He answered, "When I was eighty I did not try to live as though I were forty, and at forty I made no effort to ape the man of twenty."

Laughter was given to us to use in scaring troubles away.

The advertising of many cigarette and food manufacturers telling of their products being sure cures for all kinds of ailments has me so confused I don't know whether to ask the advice of a druggist or a grocer about my aches and pains.

No, dear reader, you are mistaken. A "star" salesman is not one who shines nights.

It is an indication of success when others look upon us as being of some importance. It is an evidence of failure when we first assume such a feeling.

It sometimes happens that those who are complaining about business being bad are trying to market a bad product at a good price.

"Now here's what I'd do" is usually the conversational starter of those who have done nothing worth mentioning.

We profess devotion to peace and yet when it comes to erecting monuments and statues to honor national heroes we generally pick on a soldier. It seems to me that a statue of Luther Burbank or Thomas A. Edison would be more in keeping if we really believe in humanity and brotherly love. Their accomplishments should be an inspiration to all of us, so why not honor them in bronze?

I have had worlds of fellows give me positive assurance that success was "just around the corner" but no one of them has been able to tell me how near I was to the corner.

When a department head is away for a few weeks, some employee is sure to say, "The business runs along just as well when he is not here." While not always said in a complimentary way, it is however a very fine compliment. It proves that he has succeeded in building an organization to run his business, which is the real job of every employer. Automobile manufacturers build cars that others can run, and the successful executive builds a business that others can run.

I have a friend who some years ago bought an insurance policy, which at the age of fifty would give him a monthly income of quite a sum of money as long as he lives. While other employees working with him were blowing money and having a good time, he was using a small part of his salary to keep up payments in his insurance. He recently quit work that he might have a good time the rest of his life on his assured monthly income. Many of his old associates have been asked to quit work, and are facing hard times, perhaps for life. What a difference and what a lesson!

The street car that carries me between office and home runs through Twin Peaks Tunnel, which is some three miles long. In the middle of the tunnel a stop is made and passengers are lifted by elevators to the surface, several hundred feet above. Near the exit is La Honda Home for aged and infirm. Often it is interesting to study the faces of the old people who are traveling to and from the poorhouse and incidentally speculate upon their past and how they came to be where they are. One day I saw an old man sitting near me on the car. With palsied hands he drew from his pocket a little paper bag and took out a piece of candy, put it in his mouth, then closing the bag as though it contained something priceless, put it back in his pocket. As he left the car someone dropped a silver dollar in his pocket. I fancy that the discovery of that dollar was for this human derelict like finding a fortune, but I doubt whether the old man's joy over finding the dollar was as great as the joy of the giver, who by his act made a tired old soul happy for days, and I wonder if the old man on finding that dollar did not revive his childhood belief in fairies and also his shattered faith in humanity.

Wise salesmen know that when they let their buyers get to knowing them too well personally they will soon be NO-ing them out of orders.

"I was just looking around" or "I'll drop in I again" are two ways the prospective buyer has of saying to a clerk, "You are not a salesman."

We worry about the things we want to do, but can't; in the place of doing that which we could do, but don't.

Of all the young men I have talked with in reform schools and penitentiaries, no one of them ever told me that his father was a man for whom he had the greatest respect and admiration, and one he always felt free to go to for advice.

Abraham Lincoln did not get his start in life by sitting in trees, but by splitting them into fence rails.

There it is—"As I See It." Doubtless you have frequently disagreed with me, but I hope you have enjoyed reading this little book. If I have caused you to stop and think occasionally, I will consider myself amply repaid for writing it. It is by thinking, you know, that we prepare ourselves to do better work, to live cleaner lives, and to be more understanding and human in our everyday contacts at home, in the office and on the street.

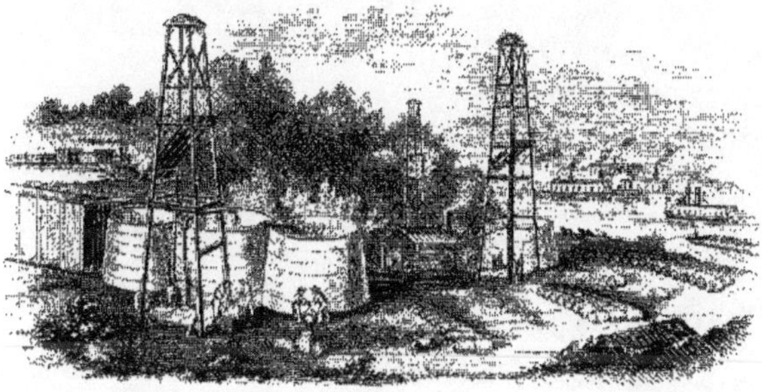

10
Here's A Good One

A slip of the foot may cause a broken limb—a slip of the tongue a broken heart.

Every man who has something against you is not pushing you forward.

You can't ease into Easy Street.

Those who think only of themselves have but little or nothing to think about.

Love may be blind but it frequently causes a fellow to see a lot of trouble he didn't know existed.

Success is built more upon Supervision than Superstition.

You can tell some men by looking at them though you couldn't tell them very much by talking to them.

Many walk into trouble with their eyes open because they are looking back on their troubles of yesterday.

It is so often the satisfying of our wants that brings us to want.

The secret of happiness comes from making others happy, but so many people advertise such acts that the secret of happiness is lost.

A slip of one negligent employee in a business can and often does nullify the work of many honest-to-goodness workers.

The difference between success and failure is no greater than the difference between Can and Can't.

Many women are shy in telling their age. Some several years shy.

When I was a youngster in school I read in McGuffy's reader that three-fourths of the earth was water. In late years I have learned from buying stock that many issues are sold in the same proportion.

It is difficult to stretch that which we know so that it will cover a thirty minute period. That is why some public speakers spend weeks in the preparation of a thirty minute talk.

Live by your wits if you will, but don't look for sympathy if someone smarter than you beats you at your own game.

A neglected duty is a committed crime.

Don't expect to be made manager of your employer's business before you have demonstrated your ability to manage yourself.

Ma and Pa found out how the "two can live as cheap as one" expression originated, when they sent Bill away to school.

Speed is not always necessary or profitable. Those who came out to California by ox team seem to have accomplished about as much as any of those who have since arrived by fast trains and aeroplanes.

A good political speaker is a man who can work his audience up to a point of becoming enthusiastic without saying anything.

No salesman can sell everyone but any salesman can sell someone.

Big thoughts are usually expressed with small words.

About as many mistakes are made in the spending of too little money as in spending too much.

Being unappreciative of what we have and envying others for what they have helps much to keep us unhappy.

Most men would succeed in their business if they did not have to take so much time from it in listening to others tell them how to run it.

As sunshine and rain make plants flourish and bloom, so industry and intelligence makes many a business yield profit and pleasure to all connected with it.

Those who pride themselves upon being as good as other men base their opinion upon the class of men they associate with, and frequently they don't amount to much.

"I don't know what becomes of my money." Brother, your creditors have long been wondering about that, too.

Somebody has said that worry makes gray heads. Maybe it does, but if so, that is about all it can claim credit for doing.

As you see yourself in a mirror is not as others see you for they are looking at your faults or virtues and reviewing your reputation.

While some men rather pride themselves on being fluent talkers, it is well to take into consideration that Calvin Coolidge perhaps does less talking than most any man, and we elected him President of the United States.

The average age of the executives of a large concern was sixty years and they voted that no man over fifty be employed because of his having outlived his usefulness.

The statement we furnish our bankers tells our financial condition, and the examination made by our physicians our physical condition, but few of us honestly invoice our morals which regulate our financial and physical condition.

The best evidence of a faulty mind is the faults it finds and expresses.

Uncertainty is but another name for Fear, and both mean Failure.

If you feel that you must tell a story then tell one that will bring a laugh and not a blush.

It is often those who are least worthy of the position they hold who think themselves worthy of something better.

It is far better to go to an attorney and pay him well for telling you what you ought to know than to personal friends who you are confident will tell you exactly what you want to hear. One is constructive advice, the other destructive flattery.

"All men are born equal." Maybe so, but equal to what or to whom remains the unanswered question.

A little business grows to be a big business because of its having won the confidence and friendship of the people. It becomes a little business again when either or both are lost.

Look ahead but do not overlook the things confronting you today.

Automobile drivers frequently do not realize how fast they are traveling until wrecked and that is often true of boys and girls.

Trying to do better than others are doing is not nearly so profitable as trying to do better than we ourselves have ever done.

Politeness pays compound interest.

Have your own ideas, but have them ready to change for those of others which you find to be better.

"Leave it to me" is seldom said to Dad when he speaks of some work to be done on the farm, but it is frequently mentioned when he says something about making his will.

An architect first makes his plans, then starts to build. All men are architects engaged in the building of their own futures and the world is becoming populated with many failures because of so few having developed any workable plan.

Know thyself, however unpleasant it may be.

The reason some people do not believe in luck is because they have never worked hard enough to enjoy any of it.

Of the two, I prefer to hear gab-bags tell what they have done, rather than what they would do if they were me.

When house organs carry less "buy-only-what-we-have-to-sell" and more "here-is-how-you-can-sell-that-which-you-have-to-sell" advice they will be better read and their publishers will sell more.

Weighting is the handicap that causes horses to lose races. Waiting is the handicap that causes salesmen to lose sales.

Life is not very long at best, which is a good reason why we shouldn't waste time in idle gossip or useless criticism of others, who are perhaps doing as well or better than we.

Short words are usually responsible for long family quarrels.

The woman who believes the man who says he would go to h-l for her usually goes with him.

Cheap merchandise is like a cheap man. Both are far too costly in the end.

Cleaning and dyeing firms advertise to remove all stains, but we know they do not mean character stains, otherwise we would all be lining up in front of their shops.

Quit looking for the kind of work you feel that you would like to do, and learn to like that which you have to do, and are perhaps better fitted for.

Money talks but it is hard of hearing. Only bankers can call it.

What some salesmen consider a "follow up" is calling on a firm after having heard of their having bought goods from a competitor who had a live-wire salesman that blazed away and blazed the way to new and profitable business.

Maybe some people do not believe in angels because they have met many who posed as such.

Being persistent without the prospective buyer finding it out is one of the arts in selling.

Some people seem to think that a good neighbor is one who keeps hammers, screw-drivers, monkey-wrenches, saws, hatchets, lawn-mowers and other things for loaning purposes only.

An advertisement is a silent salesman and therefore it cannot talk the buyer out of buying after having made a sale.

"Keep your feet on the ground" is an old saying that becomes splendid advise to farmers who want to keep mortgages off of it.

All men are Thinkers, and what they think sends some up the ladder of success, and others to penitentiaries.

A right good way to select salesmen is to employ those who sell you something you didn't want, but found you could profitably use.

Some read to be entertained, others profit by what they read. Those who become successful do both at the same time.

Those who are fair with others usually fare well.

Repentance without reformation is like a beautiful car without an engine. It will never get you anywhere.

Some of those who are finding it difficult to make ends meet have been trying to hold up their end in too fast company.

A change of environment once in a while works wonders; it makes one appreciate the good things the home town offers.

The number of wise things done is so small in comparison with the number of wise things said.

Maybe a hod-carrier never gets any place because he spends half his time in coming down. I wonder if this isn't true regarding some employees who seem stationary—same job—same pay—same petty troubles and annoyances year after year.

The race is not always to the swift or brilliant; I have seen hard plugging salesmen who would finish up the year with a much better showing than some who were higher rated.

EVERY sales manager hopes that it will be his salesmen who discover perpetual motion.

All I have to give those who lose their money in gambling or speculating is a laugh.

Pull up your chin, pull on a smile, pull off your coat, pull up your sleeves and pull for success; then you will not need the "pull" of others.

Too many young men are looking for jobs selling handkerchiefs to those who are earning a living by the sweat of their brow.

Maybe we need more ex-executives.

We are entirely wrong in assuming that only that which appeals to us will interest others. Many a piece of good merchandise has failed to become a best seller just because the salesmen did not care for it and never showed it to buyers.

The salesman who is not a pace-maker is more often an agitator than a peace-maker and he is a good man to get rid of.

A verbal understanding is all right as long as both parties continue to feel that they have the best of the bargain.

Malice is a mental cancer.

Real salesmen welcome objections. The hard-to-sell man is one who agrees with the salesman in all he says—except—when the salesman suggests he write his name on the dotted line.

When one gangster double-crosses another he is shot. What fat burying grounds we would have were the same rule carried out by all of us.

Every day there are fewer opportunities for young men who are "willing to do anything." In this day positions are filled by those who have fitted themselves to fill them.

The salesman who hurries a slow thinking prospect into making a decision seldom hurries away with an order.

The great majority of people do right and live right. Those that do not are just better advertised, that's all.

The reason we do not credit all people with having good sense is because they do not agree with us.

Unless you look out, you'll never have a look in.

Quit telling your troubles. The advertising of adversity will never bring prosperity.

"Well, I just have ten minutes to give you. What is your proposition?" And the unwise salesman tries to crowd a thirty minute solicitation into the ten minutes, which can have but one result.

The man who has experienced the wrong things can best appreciate and talk about things that are right.

Before criticizing and abusing a competitor who is doing as much or more business than you are, it is well to take into consideration the fact that the public after investigating both of you favor him.

Too many open the door of their minds to welcome scandal.

Youth dreams of the happiness to come in future years while age in memory lives over again the happiness of youth. One is hope, the other remembered reality.

Few salesmen devote enough time to selling themselves on the merchandise they are selling.

The shoemaker who loves his business is one man whose love is lasting.

Bluffs are made to hide fear or weakness.

Perhaps the reason more advertising is not sold is that by the time many advertising salesmen get through telling about the worthlessness of all other mediums, the prospect has no time left to listen to what they might have to say about the merits of their own medium. Knockers knock only themselves.

There are many roads a successful man can take to become a failure, but there is only one route the failure can travel to reach success and the milestones along that way are Truth, Honesty, Self Sacrifice and Determination.

You must first convince others that there is something in you before you can expect to get anything out of them.

No man is in the pink of condition who is green with jealousy.

Many a career has been spoiled by a carouse.

A clerk whose discourtesy causes customers to quit a store paves the way for being asked to do the same thing.

Getting a prospect's "yes" today means more to a sales manager than a salesman's talk on his success of yes-terday.

One of our best grand opera singers had just finished singing "My Old Kentucky Home" when a gentleman of perhaps eighty years turned to me and said, "She sang it right well, but nothing like as well as my wife used to sing it right up until the time of her death." Right or wrong, God bless him; I loved him for thinking so.

I have no sympathetic tears to shed for the man who is enjoying good health and the comforts of life and yet recites hard luck stories.

Common sense is very uncommon. It is only used by the more successful.

Wonder how many marriages there would be if men were as pure and had the same lovable dispositions they expect women to have.

Most so called super-salesmen I have met won their reputations by selling a wanted product that was produced by a firm which enjoyed the confidence of the buyers.

Sometime ago dozens of policemen and detectives guarded one of the world's richest men during business hours and watched over him while he slept that no harm might come to him. As I read it in the morning paper I called to mind the many good friends far and near who had called on me at my humble office during that day, and of the usual nine hours sleep I enjoyed that night, and then I could but wonder which of us was really rich.

During my many years in selling I have known far more young men to apply for positions as salesmen because it looked like an easy way of making a living than because they believed themselves fitted for the work.

Some women are a credit to their husbands as long as their husband's credit lasts.

"Doesn't he look nice and slouchy" is an expression I have never heard used even about college students.

A pessimist is a man who takes the advice of an optimist, and an optimist is a fellow who takes the pessimist's money.

Knowing much about other people is less profitable to us than knowing more than the other people know.

Just heard of a lady having shot a "Peeping Tom" who she saw at her bedroom window, and it gave me a fine idea as to what to do to salesmen calling on me whose minds are so centered on reading the correspondence on my desk that they forget what they are selling.

When nations, firms and individuals quit looking after their own affairs, their business and the living of their own lives we can well expect a national, business and mental depression.

Some of the best talks ever heard on thrift and temperance were made by men who had been spendthrifts and drunkards.

The criticisms of failures are among the first things that successful men must learn to not give a darn about.

There is a reason for all things but many of us do not stop to reason.

My list of salesmen who have failed is headed by those who jump around from one place to another looking for those who might be easy to sell.

It is not so much what you know, as what you profit by knowing. There is not a man or woman in prison but knows the Golden Rule and all are there for having violated it.

The higher education we hear so much about is nothing more than the right application of a college education to a business problem.

The unexpected usually happens and therefore we have successful men and failures. Nothing is more convincing of this than the calling to mind of our old schoolmates.

Nearly all petroleum and sugar is refined. I have met quite a few people who were not.

Nearly any inmate of a poor-house will tell you of the reputation he once had of being a good fellow, a good spender and good hearted.

There is a considerable difference between making ourselves popular and making ourselves common.

Another good form of life insurance is the learning of a trade.

Travel is an education. Each and every trip causes us to appreciate our homes and our friends more and more.

One thing that has saved the youth of today has been Dad's not confining himself strictly to the truth in delivering his "When I was a boy" oration.

Those who keep up with, or a little ahead of the times seldom see hard times.

Equally important with believing in God is giving Him reason for believing in us.

I am never an attentive listener to those having unkind things to say about others because I am wondering what they are going to say about me as soon as they find a listener.

Every well-to-do man is a will-to-do man.

Uncle Sam could make the Post Office pay big money were he to charge double postage on "please remit" mail.

It is always the customer who is making the most unjust complaint that appears the most angry and talks the loudest.

He had a cheese factory and was doing a big business. He invested his profits in steel and oil stocks about which he knew nothing, and lost his money. He immediately quit advertising his cheese, reduced his sales force and discharged many other employees hoping to regain his losses and that wrecked his cheese business.

We look upon others as being unreasonable because they do not agree with us, while the world accepts them as being wise.

A salesman should not only believe in himself, but believe himself.

Expressions, actions and deeds are so often backed up with the "ax-to-grind" idea that we long to meet a real honest man.

The country could get along better with fewer mental undertakers.

Every man educates himself. All school can do is to prepare him for the undertaking.

There are perhaps very few things listed on a menu that appeal to the manager of the hotel. A menu must offer things that appeal to everyone. Many hotel managers have found it profitable to use advertising that others would be interested in reading rather than that which appeals only to them. P.S. Others than hotel men might profit by the idea.

We profit more by accepting that which we lack than that which we like.

Uncle Billy Wise once said, "They laugh at me for saying 'git,' but I have noticed that the fellow that 'gits' up early, and 'gits' on the job ahead of the others usually 'gits' what he is after."

The saving of earnings, means the saving of yearnings.

Too many young men in choosing a calling hear only the call of the wild, wild company.

An employee's first start for failure is when he becomes satisfied with doing as well as those who are working with him.

Few of those living on Easy Street have lifetime leases.

A farmer first prepares his soil, then he sows the seed. A good salesman will prepare the prospect to receive his solicitation before he makes it.

An echo is never so loud as the original noise and it is too bad that the same cannot be said about repeated scandal.

It is not the sweat of the brow that produces a highbrow but the personal appraisement of a lowbrow.

No man has ever suffered the loss of a real friend except by death.

If a young man were to go about his work with the same enthusiasm as he does in arranging for his vacation his success would be assured.

Buck-up—don't back-up.

Many so called conservative men are just ordinary fellows without any initiative whatever who are suffering from a severe case of procrastination brought on by fear.

The man who thinks himself alone when not in company with others is not a thinker. Because he is not being a thinker may explain why others leave him alone.

Imagination, solicitation, then realization. A good salesman excites a man's imagination about driving a new car, owning a home, wearing a new suit or drinking a good cup of coffee. Then follows his convincing solicitation which results in the realization.

Those in selling who have missed their calling are those who make the fewest calls.

There is the good man and the self-believed good looking man. One is adorable—the other deplorable.

Those who foresee adversity seldom see it.

"A half a loaf is better than no loaf at all" is an old maxim, but in these days of modern business those who succeed do not loaf at all.

The most unselfish of all people are school teachers who prepare others to go into the world to make reputations and gain wealth, while they keep on being teachers, at small pay.

Often when the sale has been made and the buyer is ready to place an order, fear overtakes the salesman and he starts a new line of talk that causes the buyer to change his mind and the order is lost.

Unlike bankers, ice cream manufacturers advertise their frozen assets and sell them at a profit.

Quit making liars out of people by asking them to tell you just what they think of you or your business.

A person with a bad memory is one who remembers only the bad he sees in others and does not remember the bad he has done others.

If you don't win, don't whine.

Being able to read is the key that unlocks the treasure chest and gives us the thoughts of the wise men of the world that we may profitably make use of them.

It is just too bad that the unemployed list is not headed by crepe hangers, gossipers and scandalmongers.

One night of foolishness often destroys all that was accomplished by years of carefulness.

Some of the most convincing salesmen are out of jobs because they have convinced their sales managers they could not sell.

Singers make a reputation by singing songs that please their hearers and then wreck their reputation by singing songs that are most pleasing to themselves.

Enjoy a little Heaven before you die as it may be your last chance.

The best memorandum the head of many concerns could pass out to all departments would be, "There will be no more memorandums."

Opportunity is most considerate. It does not pull the lazy out of their beds nor does it go to matinees and ball parks looking for those who are supposed to be at work.

Some people have an idea that what they don't know is not worth knowing. And what they do know is not worth knowing, according to what others think.

"Love, honor and obey" has been eliminated by some ministers in the performing of marriage ceremonies. However that has nothing to do with employees loving their work, honoring their employees and obeying instructions.

There is only one way to escape remaining a wage earner and that is to earn more than your wages.

There is no better recommendation than a good reputation.

The best way to correct a fault is to admit it.

Thinking only of ourselves is another way of increasing our unhappiness. The more we see of others the more we appreciate that which we are and that which we have.

A friend was telling me that he had never worked a cross-word puzzle, but he was working for one, and married to another.

Prize-fighting may not be the most noble calling, but the combatants, anyhow, face each other to deal out punishment which, to me, seems more man-like than passing out character killing blows when somebody's back is turned.

It is friction that destroys machinery and a sales organization or an office force might as well be looked upon as a machine.

I have met many star salesmen. Some of them were rising stars, while others were sitting stars.

Few depressions have been known that deprived men of their vices.

Our first day at school teaches us that we must learn from others and that one important lesson should go along with us through life.

I haven't noticed so very much difference between egotism and idiotism.

Maybe the reason a bagpipe player always walks while playing is so he may be ready to run in case his listeners start throwing things his way. Sooner or later saxophone players will use the same good judgment.

In front of a store that daily offered its merchandise at less than actual cost stood a man who was giving his money away to passers-by. He was arrested and proved to be of unsound mind.

Luther Burbank once said to me, "I dislike being called a wizard." Mr. Edison told me he did not consider himself a genius. Both said they attributed their success to plain hard work.

The seat of success is not always a swivel chair.

When you are honest and truthful with yourself and your fellow man you are the equal of any man you may meet and fear will then have no place in your mind.

Taking from the top drawer of his desk a dozen or more charts covered with curves and figures which had been prepared by some efficiency expert the president of a big concern proceeded to explain them to a caller. After a thirty minute oration he turned to the caller and asked, "Well, what do you think of them?" The caller answered, "The one thought that was going through my mind the first fifteen minutes was, I don't know what the h-l he is talking about. And for the last fifteen minutes my thought has been, he doesn't know what the h-l he is talking about."

Mighty few men ever do their jobs and get a hundred per cent result, but that doesn't argue that we should give up trying.

Poor people being in the majority, this old world is a pretty happy sort of a place in which to live after all.

The thoughts of others are only valuable to us when they cause us to think for ourselves. It is our own thoughts that guide us to failure or success.

Some business men will keep stenographers after hours to get out letters of importance and then to save three cents postage will send the letter regular mail in the place of air mail, delaying its delivery three days.

My list of best liars is headed with those who say they never worry about anything.

Fortunately the opinions others have of us are based upon the little they know about us and not on what we know about ourselves.

I am always a little afraid of the man who neither smiles nor laughs.

Husbands and eggs become hard-boiled if kept in hot water.

Unless a salesman sells the first man he sees in the morning he need not hold out much hope of selling others he is to see during the day. The first man he sees will appear in his mirror.

When you think your job is just going round and round in circles, consider the merry-go-round of your childhood days. It made many children happy and some money for its operator.

Being reasonably dumb is not half so bad as being too smart with a good customer.

Fifteen years ago, I read a verse from "Rhymes Without Reason" that I have always remembered:

"The wisest men
That e'er you ken
Have never deemed it treason
To rest a bit
And jest a bit
And balance up their reason;
To laugh a bit
And chaff a bit
And joke a bit in season."

If I've made you smile a bit and laugh a bit, stop a bit and think a bit—then I will not be accused of undue boldness for having said, "Here's a Good One," and life will go on being happy for me.

Index

www.ingramcontent.com/pod-product-compliance
Lightning Source LLC
Chambersburg PA
CBHW021852020426
42334CB00013B/299
* 9 7 8 0 9 7 6 3 7 6 0 3 3 *